A Jar of Treacle

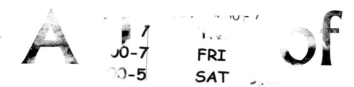

Macclesfield Memories

"Some secretary— she promised to get stuck into this back-log of mail!"

Geoffrey Hunter

To
Claire Isabel Crosbie
in gratitude

ACKNOWLEDGMENTS

In his most generous foreword to this book, Doug Pickford writes of his 'open door' policy as an editor and how when we met for the first time - it was in July 1992 incidentally - we bonded immediately. Doug's amiability was the reason for the magic; I might have been a valued old friend rather than the total stranger I, in fact, was. This initial meeting and instant friendship resulted in my book *Waterloo Boy* being published in 1996, thanks to Doug and his 'open sesame' access to publisher Bruce Richardson, who accorded me the same spontaneous warmth.

Since then, with the launch of the Old Macc magazine, of which Doug's wife Hilary is editor, I have become even closer to his family. Add to this list dear Claire Crosbie who has been a constant influence in my life since 1973. Claire has not only been adviser in the creation of my two books, but an over-worked word-processor operator in this latest venture.

To this quartet go my eternal thanks.

Of a host of friends I must mention the following who have helped in some special way:

Margaret Burgess, Adelene L. Cage, Marion Swindells, John Sutton, Ken Miller, Len Billington, Keith Mason, Heather Jobling, Brenda Bailey, Gerald Bradley, Lynne Smith and The Mail Box, Park Green. Grateful thanks to all.

CHURNET VALLEY BOOKS
1 King Street, Leek, Staffordshire ST13 5NW 01538 399033
www.leekbooks.co.uk
© Geoff Hunter and Churnet Valley Books 2005
ISBN 1 904546 35 8

Foreword

By Doug Pickford

Editor of the Macclesfield Express 1972-1997

When I was editor of the Macclesfield Express I had an 'open door' policy - anyone could come into the office and have a word. After all, I never knew what lay ahead and what marvellous people I would meet.

One day the receptionist telephoned me. *"There's a Mr Hunter here. He would like to speak to you."*

"Send him in."

That was it.

I am pleased to relate that from that day (quite some years ago now) to this we have been firm friends with a mutual bond - our love of Macclesfield. We make a point of meeting up regularly at a local hostelry, Geoff with Claire, and I with Hilary, and it is always when the pub is holding its quiz night. We always fall down badly on the pop music questions but, if the learned quizmaster ever chose to ask questions on Old Macc, we would win hands down with Geoffrey's indefatigable knowledge; but he doesn't!

Geoffrey Hunter has taught me a lot. Not least, he has shown me what a joyous experience anticipation can be: that act of looking forward to an event and living it, over and over again, within your imagination before actually experiencing it. He passed this on to me when initially relating his delightful tale of when Pinocchio, the Walt Disney full-length cartoon film, first came to the Majestic in Mill Street, and how he waited until Saturday night to see it - so he could anticipate the event throughout the week. How this story ends has now gone down in the annals of Macclesfield's history.

He also taught me a lot about Macclesfield of yesteryear and, even more importantly, how delightful yesteryear was.

It's not, and never has been, a matter of re-living those Good Old Days, if they ever existed. No it is a matter of appreciating what we had, who was there, and what we were taught and experienced. It's a matter of taking a delight in the simple things of life, the ordinary everyday events that we took for granted and now wish we could re-live.

Geoffrey Hunter is no ordinary man. He won't thank me for saying this, for he is a modest person by nature, but he has been an exceptional winner of competitions in his heyday; he has been a devoted family man; an artist whose work has been appreciated by Her Majesty Queen Elizabeth II and more recently, an author whose first work *Waterloo Boy* took his home town by storm. Needless to say, it's now sold out.

So it is with absolute delight I can anticipate this, his new work *A Tang of Treacle*, an enchanting title for a book written by a true Son of Macclesfield.

Macclesfield Express 1962

CONTENTS

GEOFFREY HUNTER
Here seen editing Frank Burgess's story (Chapter 32),
'an absorbing and joyous exercise'.

1

A Backwards Glance

In 1996 when I had completed the writing of *Waterloo Boy* I had traversed the first eighteen years of my life, from my birth, over the shop at 87 Mill Street, Macclesfield in 1927, until being conscripted 'For the Duration of National Emergency', in July, 1945.

At the time I joined the Army the war in Europe was over but hostilities against Japan seemed destined to last some considerable time. I recall that during my first few weeks of primary training at Gallowgate Camp, Richmond, Yorkshire, there were, dotted about the camp, incomprehensible signs displaying Japanese writing as if to acclimatise us for Far Eastern parts, and the Camp Padre preached to us of the glory of after-life!

We now know that President Truman and a few of his closest friends knew more than the ordinary man in the street when he approved the dropping of two atom bombs on Japan during August that year. The rest, as they say is history.

It was at this point that 'Waterloo Boy' reached its conclusion. It had given me considerable pleasure to write and the Macclesfield public had been so supportive I will be forever grateful to all concerned for the warmth generated by the book's reception.

A most pleasing feature was the number of people who wrote to me and in the kindest way. I have selected one such letter from Mr Len Billington of Manchester whose father was a very close friend of mine and a most generous man to my family.

12.2.97

Dear Mr Hunter,

I received your book 'Waterloo Boy' as a Christmas gift from my brother, and have only now started to get my teeth into it!

Before carrying on I think it is in order to put myself into context. My Auntie Nellie (Worthington, nee Billington) lived for many years at 62, Fence Street with Stan her husband, a really keen gardener! You mention Geoffrey, their son, in your book. My father, Jim, was Nellie's youngest sibling. Their

A recent Mill Street photograph showing the imposing edifice of the former Majestic cinema on the left, and, on the extreme right, number 87, believed to be a grocer's when Geoffrey was born in a room over the shop in 1927.

Cotton Street children's party, 1958. Geoff's children, Lorraine and Paul on the left.

Daybrook Street Boys' School where Geoffrey was educated before moving to Central School in the late thirties.

elder sister, Alice, married Tommy Cundiff of Black Road Post Office, and indeed the Close where the shop used to be is now named Cundiffe's Close.

I arrived in Macclesfield in the early fifties, and during the first weekend, I met two young lads who went to the Central School, where I was due to start the following Monday, joining the third year. We went shopping in Chestergate, where I was amazed and delighted to discover the Army and Navy Store. I purchased a 'bomber' jacket, the likes of which I had never seen before. My new found friends assured me that it would be OK to wear it for school, as the uniform wasn't essential!

Next day my friends took me scrumping for apples, a game I could at least match them in, having been born and brought up in Barnton, then a very rural village, literally surrounded by apple trees.

We 'collected' quite a few, and my friends suggested I take some to school to share with their friends. I did. Due to getting lost and just plain dawdling, I arrived late for assembly. Conducted by R.E. Houseman himself.

"THAT BOY", Houseman virtually bawled like an RSM on the parade ground. "COME!"

A pleasant teacher guided me onto the stage from which Houseman was conducting affairs, and I stood in bewilderment at his extraordinary facial twitching, and the unmistakable buzz from the rest of the pupils. It hit me in the pit of my stomach to realise, as I gazed at the rank upon rank of uniformed boys, that I must look pretty odd. Not improved by the fact I had ingeniously hidden the apples in the 'bomber' jacket, "I know you, Pilkington", Houseman stuttered and stammered, "I know you".

"My name is Billington, sir."

"As ever, arguing, eh LAD?" He glared at me. "What are you wearing?"

"Bomber jacket, sir." My joy was fading fast.

"Come here," he yelled, and as soon as I got close enough, he yanked my jacket open.

As long as I was at Central School, I never heard again the spontaneous cheering that swelled from my fellow pupils as the apples cascaded around me.

"To my office, Pilkington, at once."

And so started two years of purgatory from this man, who for ever after called me Pilkington - and if I argued I wasn't, Houseman would send me to his office for arguing, and if I didn't deny it, I was sent to his office because I was Pilkington! The only saving grace was he had become quite infirm and weak, and his caning was quite erratic, as he often used his left hand, swinging the cane from his right shoulder, and hitting me anywhere along my outstretched arm, my shoulder and even my head!

Thank goodness there was no power in his swipes at me. I estimated I paid him twenty such visits. Why the rest of the staff let this carry on, I, to this day don't understand. I kept my Dad out of it because it wasn't painful, and I knew what Dad could do when his passions were aroused (he quelled a deranged cow that was going to gore us children by grabbing its horns and throwing it to the floor. Houseman wouldn't have stood a chance!!)

So you can imagine how many memories your book has stirred of this - in my book hateful - man. Not least is the day 'Big Harry' left school. Houseman had tried to bully Harry for years, probably because he was big, and this horrid little man felt a need to show who was 'biggest'. Walking out of the school building for the very last time, Harry headed for the bike shed, and to a certain funny little car in there! He was accompanied by several other leavers. As happens in schools, the word had got about that something was to happen, but what we didn't know, so obviously we hung about in keen anticipation. And it was well worth it. They tipped Houseman's car onto its roof, and walked away, quite calmly. We didn't, we scarpered, real fast!

So thank you and well done! I felt almost compelled to share my memories of Houseman with someone else, and there you are! (Mind you, the 'Pilkington' story is quite well known in my family!)

> *Yours sincerely,*
> *Len Billington*

Waterloo Boy was entirely autobiographical, and now that I am putting pen to paper once again I wish the reader to know I intend to continue writing of my own experiences, from my return to Civvy Street and my life throughout the fifties, particularly my years in Cotton Street, memories very close to my heart.

Beyond that point I hope to offer readers a mixed-bag of tales, all with a Macclesfield flavour.

2

Back to Civvy Street

When I was demobbed from the Army in July 1948, after three years service, I had good reason to be pleased. The previous year I had gambled on my chances of being back home for the Olympic Games in London - the first 'Games' to be held since 1936 in Berlin - and had booked to attend the entire athletics programme. I don't recall the sum involved but I regarded it as modest, and here I was, back in Macclesfield with a week to spare!

But that was not the only blessing. Within a few days the trepidation I had felt in regard to job-seeking was resolved in the easiest way. I met up with an old pal, John Challinor of Nicholson Avenue and we were discussing my return to normality. I mentioned that within the Army I had burgeoned as a budding cartoonist but what success I had had so far did not indicate it was likely to put much bread on my table.

"Take your cartoons down to Barracks - you'll get a job in their designing room," he said.

Now Barracks Fabrics, Lower Heys, was well known to me. Dad, my sister Eileen, and brother Vincent had each worked there in the past but it was a fabric printing company. Taking cartoons there to seek employment seemed illogical, and I said so. John had an answer to that too.

"You're not going there to sell cartoons. You're going to sell yourself. I've worked at Barracks and I know what is done in their designing room. What they look for in a newcomer is aptitude, pure and simple. Once you're in, they'll mould you in the way they want."

I mentioned the conversation to Dad when I returned home. *"If you want an appointment with Mr Hermon, it's no sooner said than done. Let's just say he's grateful to me for helping him out in the past."*

And so, a couple of days later I presented myself to Mr H.G. Hermon, founder of the company and Managing Director. *"Let's see what you've brought with you"*. I unfolded my brown-paper parcel of six cartoons.

"Mmmm... where did you copy these from then?" he asked.

"I've not copied them from anywhere", I replied. *"If you'd like me to draw you one right now I'd be pleased to do so"*. He waved his hands

dismissively. *"No need for that. You can start next Monday at 8.30am. I'll pay you £4.10s per week"*.

I pointed out that I would be unable to start that soon and explained my Olympic gamble. *"With your permission , sir, I'd like to start a fortnight later, if you don't mind"*.

"That'll suit me fine. I wouldn't want you to miss all that Olympic excitement; but I can't help thinking", he mused *"that a young man like you should be seeking work more suitable to your talent. I'm not without influence in Fleet Street; I'll certainly sound out the possibility of getting you on a paper as cartoonist. In the meantime, you'll be working for me. Give my regards to your father"*.

So now I could travel to the London Olympics knowing I'd got a job to come back to. Full marks to John Challinor!

That summer I spent 10 days in Chiswick staying with my sister Eileen and her husband George. Actually the XIII Olympiad of 1944 had been awarded to London in 1938 but, as war intervened London was made host of the X1V Olympiad. Coming so soon after hostilities, inevitably the event was an austere affair. Competitors were housed in former service huts and catering was nothing like the pampered sports stars of today would expect. Even so, it was a genuine and gallant attempt by London to 'get back to normal' and they deserve full credit for what they achieved.

The Olympic athletic programme was a splendid sporting pageant I wouldn't have missed for the world. Each of my tickets entitled me to a seat for a full day each morning I entered Wembley Stadium. Today one's ticket would probably qualify you for a seat for a portion of the morning!

The star of the show was 30-year-old mother-of-two, Fanny Blankers-Koen a Dutch sprinter, who collected four gold medals. Czech, Emil Zatopek gained his first Olympic gold in the 10,000 metres.

In addition to seeing the world's finest athletes perform I found time to take in a matinee at the London Palladium where the Andrews Sisters were booked for a season and one evening I danced at the Hammersmith Palais to Lou Preager and his band playing 'Dance, Ballerina, Dance' and other hits of the day.

Returning to Macclesfield, my own challenge lay before me... My first day at Barracks Fabrics was, you might say, a pleasant baptism. I was introduced to the other members of staff and allocated a desk, and the working programme explained to me. There was no danger of my being 'thrown in at the deep end' as there was much mundane work to keep me busy while my confidence increased. A very fair system prevailed.

Staff members included Mr Bill McCulloch, head designer; Mr J.H. (Harry) Jones, Studio Manager, and artists Walter Potts, Bill Dent, Dorothy Harris, George Davenport DFM, May Hirst, Harold Yarwood, George Irving and John Scoggins, a talented teenager. In total, I believe there were about twenty employed in the designing room at that time.

1949, I learned, was the firm's Silver Jubilee year and plans to celebrate were already under way with the Macclesfield Arms as venue. Employees were being asked to contribute money towards gifts for Mr Hermon and his wife. The Barracks staff contributed separately to the purchase of a silver salver, designed by Mr Jones, which incorporated each staff member's name, and very nice it was too. The main workforce's gift was an oil-painted copy of a photograph of Mr Hermon and an antique brooch for his wife.

It was some celebration party. Several hundred were employed at Barracks in those days of hand-screen and hand-block printing, and one incident at the party comes to mind. We had dined, speeches had been made and gifts presented. Mr Hermon's portrait was of a size which all could see but his wife's brooch, of which she was so proud to be the recipient was different, resting on its velvety bed within the box that had been chosen as worthy of the role it was to play.

Mrs Hermon was eager for each guest to peruse the subject of her enchantment and suggested a sequence of movement for the bauble to pass from hand to hand and table to table, and it set off on its journey on table one, whether in its box or not I cannot say.

From this point on the company, generally, was smoking and drinking freely and it was quite some time before Mrs Hermon let her top-table guests know of the discomfort she was feeling in not having had her brooch returned to her. Immediately, a loud voice called for order. Mrs Hermon's brooch should have been returned to her long ago. Could the person currently in possession of it, the top table voice asked, announce its location? Total silence. Oh, dear!

At that stage, I dare say, the aggrieved Mrs H. took great comfort in the knowledge that the Police Station in Churchside was a mere hundred yards away, but common sense prevailed. A top-table guest was appointed to go to the the starting point of the brooch's journey and commence asking the question, *"Did you see the brooch?... Did you see the brooch?..."* and so on.

Eventually, still at the first table, the sequence of affirmative answers to the question changed when a bleary-eyed printer answered *"What brooch?,"* and when the next man confirmed he had yet to see it, the indications were that the culprit had been found. His questioning called for discretion: *"We think that perhaps you - er - may have - er - absent-mindedly, you understand have put Mrs Hermon's brooch in - er - your coat pocket. Would you be a good chap, if you don't mind, and feel - ?"* Fortunately, the man was in a blissful state and happy to do anything to oblige. He felt in both side pockets of his coat at the same time, suddenly frowned and withdrew a hand containing the missing brooch. At this point he was lost for words and smiled - or grimaced - sheepishly.

No harm had been done. In truth the incident had produced patches of laughter and the odd guffaw. A greater truth was that it had been a 'hiccup' the evening could well have done without and Mrs Hermon was relieved to have the brooch back in her possession.

3

The Actor

During the second half of 1948 at Barracks Fabrics, there was an unusually large printing order of an attractive head-square called the 'Hamlet' scarf. It was a seven colour design and such was its importance, there was always a duplicate set of silk screens available should any one screen suffer damage. This valuable printing order had come to Barracks purely by accident.

On one of his frequent business trips to London - Barracks had an office in Argyle Street which also houses the London Palladium - Mr Hermon socialising one evening chanced to meet up with an actor who was, in thespian language, 'resting'. On hearing of Mr Hermon's textile printing business the actor, who appeared to be in his mid-thirties disclosed that he had for some time been musing over an idea for a head-square design. Taking an empty cigarette packet from an ash-tray and gently tearing it open, he demonstrated with his pen on the inside surface exactly what he had in mind.

Clearly Mr Hermon was impressed, for he invited the actor, Peter, to come to the factory at Lower Heys for a couple of weeks to paint his design. The offer was accepted and during the next fortnight, Peter demonstrated a remarkable artistic ability producing his 'Hamlet' scarf, depicting the various characters from this Shakespearean tragedy with short quotations from the play printed in Old English script around the four edges.

"Stay with me!" pleaded Mr Hermon, knowing an asset when he saw one. But Peter declined.

"I'll pay you £20 a week!" insisted H.G.H.

At this time such a sum was indeed princely, by Macclesfield standards, but again the offer was refused, Peter preferring to continue in the profession he loved.

A quiet and unassuming man during his stay at Barracks, Peter's stature as an actor went largely unrecognised. Far from being an unknown actor he had already enjoyed some years' success in Hollywood, having appeared in *The Man in the Iron Mask* with Louis Hayward and Joan Bennett in 1939, with Laurel and Hardy in *A Chump at Oxford* in the same year, and in 1940, opposite Carol Lombard in a nursing drama, *Vigil in the Night*, and three other films. Some pedigree!

In 1947 he returned to this country to play Osric in *Hamlet*, starring Laurence Olivier - which explains the head-square.

The actor's full name? In later years he was to become Master of the Macabre. None other than Peter Cushing of Hammer Films fame. He was wise in refusing Mr Hermon's £20 a week. He averaged two films a year for the next forty years.

4

Settling In

Life at Barracks Fabrics wasn't all about work, as was shown early in the next year with the Silver Jubilee party at the Macclesfield Arms. Mr Hermon, known as Pete to his friends, provided social events for his workers. That August we had a Saturday train trip to Blackpool with a bit of pocket money provided. Those were the days when Blackpool were a footballing force in the first division and Matthews and Mortenson were a regular double act at Bloomfield Road, and many of our people saw them that day.

Christmas too was a good time to be at Barracks. Beer would be provided for the workers on the afternoon before we closed for Christmas Day and Boxing Day and at some point near to Christmas we would party in the work's canteen when Frankie Woods and Tiny Little, entertainers who worked at the factory, would do their stuff. In later years, entertainers were brought in from 'outside'.

Whilst I think of it, the prospect of my moving to a Fleet Street newspaper, mooted by Mr Hermon at my job interview, was never mentioned again. An important feature of HGH's leadership is that almost every day he called in the designing room and walked and paused to see what each one of our number was doing. You knew if he had nothing to say, he approved. He knew each stage of the work and would be quick to comment when necessary: *"Why are you filling in that blotch with such a small brush? For God's sake get a number six between your fingers - you'll do it in a fraction of the time"*.

I didn't know it initially but as time went on his study of my work would occasionally result in an extra five shillings in my pay packet, come next pay day, and on reflection, on numerous occasions, I was content knowing Mr H was controlling my destiny.

In the autumn of 1948 I joined Macclesfield Harriers and with the coming of winter became a member of the Liberal Club, Queen Victoria Street. These decisions proved to be very good moves on my part and, I might say, incredibly cheap as a participant. I think I paid a few pence weekly towards the harriers' changing-room rent of London Road Sunday School and eight shilling per YEAR subscription to the Liberals!

The big plus was that from both pursuits I netted about 50 new staunch friends, and I could name them all if my intention was to bore you.

About this time too, I started courting Dorothy, the five cinemas in the town being our main courting areas.

1949 saw Barracks Fabrics strengthening its designing room staff with fresh young blood from Central School: Donald Fairfoot, Graham Arthur and Gordon Lennard were promising 16-year-olds and we welcomed a mature artist from Morecambe, Tom Molyneux (who planted his roots firmly in town, raised a family with his wife 'Mac' and they are here to this day). Les Anderton was another innovative artist who joined us soon afterwards, arriving on his motor-cycle daily from Manchester.

Macclesfield Harriers Dance at the Stanley Hall about 1950.
L to R: Mr Welch (treasurer), Fred Culley, Albert Rigby, John Norton, Jim Mottershead, Joe Smith, Geoffrey Hunter, Jim Bamford

Early in the fifties another youngster to join us was Colin Holloway, one of a new breed of swimming stars of that era.

On 30th March, 1952, Dorothy and I were married at St. Peter's Church. We were supposed to have a small cottage house to move into but were gazumped as our wedding day neared. 'Gazumped' wasn't in my vocabulary at the time - I think the word I used was 'diddled', and I was very angry, having shaken hands on the deal.

However, ultimately it proved to have been a lucky escape for us, perhaps in more ways than one, when the gable-end of our once-intended home collapsed!

At the time we were married I was earning £6.10s.0d a week and Dorothy a very small wage from Smales. Our honeymoon was 4 days at the Sherwood Hotel, Reads Avenue, Blackpool, after which Dorothy moved back with her mother with me in tow! Admittedly, it wasn't what we had planned, but it was a simple answer to our dilemma and it worked out reasonably well. Our son Paul was born there 18 months later...

5

A Sporting Challenge

The early 1950s were so filled with interest for me that I'm having to think carefully about establishing the correct sequence.

I believe that the two stories that I recall now concerning Barracks colleague Colin Holloway occurred when Colin was still a teenager and I was still living at my wife's family home in Black Road.

One particular day we were touching up negatives in the dark room.

Since Colin was a renowned sprint swimmer, champion of Macclesfield Borough and of an area well beyond its boundaries, and I an enthusiastic if less gifted athlete with Macclesfield Harriers, inevitably we discussed sporting prowess.

"How long does it take you to swim the 25 yards length of Macc baths?" I asked, recalling my own laboured efforts in the same pool over the years. *"Less than 12 seconds,"* was Colin's confident reply. I was impressed by this, and a wee bit dubious.

Geoffrey (with woollen hat) and Harrier pals at London Road Sunday School prior to a training run, about 1952.

Photo includes: Mr Welch, Selwyn Watton, Joe Smith, Arthur Evans, Jack Lea, Michael Lafferty, Fred Culley, Dennis Clayton, Derek Sims, Frank Gratton, Stan Cooke, Peter Dunlop, Graham Wright, Joe Ware

"That's about the time it takes me to run up the 108 Steps", I mused. Now it was Colin's turn to be dubious and other voices of scepticism sounded. A challenge with a half-crown wager was made and accepted and as arrangements were made to stage the two separate events interest was generated by the sheer unpredictability of the outcome.

It was agreed the challenge would be staged on two successive Wednesday lunch-times between 12.30 and 1pm which would allow participants and spectators alike time for some lunch afterwards. Colin would do his swim on the first Wednesday without benefit of a dive, starting in the water with one hand on the rail. I would toe the bottom step for my run a week later without benefit of run-up impetus. The starter was to be Mr John Scoggins of Clowes Street and timekeeper Mr Les Anderton of Manchester, who many will remember as a Ministry of Transport driving examiner in later years.

Each recorded time was to remain secret until all parties had returned to Barracks Fabrics following phase two, when the result would be announced by Les at the commencement of the afternoon work period.

Since the sporting disciplines were totally different, I must stress, in fairness to Colin, the challenge was not to determine the better man but an attempt to classify the respective difficulty of each event.

That first Wednesday, our party - all designing room personnel - paid for admission to the public baths.

The baths were then in Davenport Street, and we watched Colin prepare for the first phase. After a gentle warm-up in the water he positioned himself at the deep end, one hand gripping the rail, the other arm outstretched, and his feet high up on the tiles. At the 'off' with the first few rapid strokes I was reminded of the experiment in the Central School lab, years before, when Mr Francis, the chemistry master, had deposited a morsel of sodium on the surface of a bowl of water and we watched it go berserk! The water seemed to boil as Colin sped along that length. We were all in awe of his performance as Les Anderton recorded the time in his note-book.

A week later it was my turn. I took my harrier's kit to work that day and having changed into it at lunch-time, jogged my way to the 108 Steps. Word had got around and there were more spectators this time. Dear old pal Fred Holland, also a harrier, had come from his work at Scragg's, Sunderland Street, to support me and took up his position with time-keeper Les at the top of the steps.

Starter John stood at the junction of Short Street, part way up the steps, with a raised handkerchief, visible from the top and bottom. My left foot toed the bottom step. When the hanky dropped I knew from practice what was needed. To keep my sights high searching for the top all the way and to forget the steps existed. They were so worn and rounded in the centre it was safe to treat this 55 yards upward dash as a gentle, undulating path.I was surprised how easy it was without the restriction of long trousers and I was still accelerating when I hit the top step. But had I done enough? We all returned to work for lunch and Les's announcement was eagerly awaited.

"Colin Holloway." he stated, *"Eleven point five seconds."* This feat earned Colin a generous round of applause. More applause followed when he announced: *"Geoff Hunter, ten point seven seconds."* Which proved beyond any doubt, that Colin had had much the harder task.

A few words of warning are in order at this point: most local people will know that in more recent times the 108 Steps have been completely reconstructed. Each new stone step has been given a true level and the risers have a height of up to six inches. Each step now has a sharp edge of shin-bone cracking potential. It would be madness for anyone to attempt a dash up the steps today with the abandonment I was able to display with impunity, all those years ago.

There is a second story concerning Colin and myself of that same period and although it is a story I tell against myself it is a tale worth relating.

One day, as we came to the end of the morning work period at Barracks I made a loud plea

The 108 steps from the top

for the loan of a bicycle. I needed to go into town for a new pair of shoes and I reckoned that with transport I could do the errand and have time for lunch in the firm's canteen, all within the hour. Colin responded immediately and pointed out his bike - it was an old black model which had seen better-balanced days - and I wobbled for a while as I set off with a Black Lane/Hibel Road/Jordangate route in mind. These thoroughfares were negotiated without difficulty and having passed what had been Mrs Hulme's honey shop in Jordangate and then the Macclesfield Arms, I saw ahead of me PC Gordon Bailey of Langley, an old Army Cadet pal, on point duty in the Market Place.

He was new to the Force and we exchanged greetings as he waved me past the Town Hall with a white-gloved hand.

I turned into Derby Street where Newdays Furniture Store was on one corner and the shoe shop on the other. Saxone is the name that comes to mind but accuracy is not important to this story.

Having parked the bike at the kerb I studied styles and prices in the window and reached a decision before entering the shop. I pointed out the shoes to the assistant and stated my size. In no time at all I was trying on the shoes with satisfaction. I was oblivious to the few other customers in the shop, paid the assistant and begged from him a carrier-bag for ease of carriage.

I was pleased with the speed of things. Once outside I threaded the bag onto the handlebars, manoeuvred the bike to point up Mill Street, and commenced my return journey. Gordon Bailey was still on point duty and waved me cheerily through to Jordangate. I was back at Barracks by 1pm leaving me with a half hour for lunch. I returned the bike to its spot, quickly deposited the shoes in my department, strolled down the yard to the canteen, joined Colin at his table and thanked him for his help.

I had reached the sweet course when I glanced up and was surprised to see PC Gordon Bailey striding purposefully towards me. *"Didn't expect to see you again so quickly, Gordon"*, I said. He slid into an empty chair and asked, *"Was that your bike I saw you on just now?"* I explained that the bicycle belonged to Colin. *"What's the problem, Gordon?"* I wanted to know. *"One thing at a time"*, he said. *"First, I'd like you to show me where the bike is now."* He glanced at Colin, *"I'd like you to come with us."*

The three of us strolled together up the yard to the spot where the bike was leaning against the wall just as I had left it. *"Is this your bike?"* Gordon asked Colin. Silly question, I thought, but left it to Colin to confirm. I was non-plussed when he replied, *"No"*.

I rounded on Colin. *"You told me this was your bike,"* I insisted. He shook his head. *"Not this one, I didn't"*, he countered. Completely bewildered by this I asked Gordon *"What goes on?"* He spoke authoritatively. *"I'll tell you what goes on."* He slapped the bike's saddle with his hand. *"Your backside on that seat! Get back on this bike, pedal it back to the shoe shop where you'll find your pal's bike still parked outside where you left it. But before you bring the right bike back, be good enough to go into the shop and make your apologies to Father Kelly of St. Alban's Church, who reported his bike stolen at one o'clock."*

Sheepishly I obeyed. It was with relief I found Father Kelly a most understanding and forgiving man. But then, you would expect that from a Catholic priest, wouldn't you?

6

Forebodings

When I was a greengrocer's delivery-boy in Hurdsfield just before the war, my employer, Mrs Florrie Wright treated me more like a son than a boy engaged solely to run errands. She fed me when I arrived at her shop from the Central School in the late afternoon, and during quiet periods she loved to talk to me of her past life.

She was of the Avery family of Langley, the sister of Tom and Elsie. She was a deeply religious lady and had a strong belief in the supernatural, and narrated to me personal stories of seeing ghosts, experiencing premonitions, good and bad, and told with such conviction and sincerity, I was left in no doubt that Life had its mysteries and I, in my turn, might come to witness some of them, eventually...

Of the two stories I am going to recount I have good reason to affirm the accurate dating of the second, as will become obvious in due course. The first I cannot date precisely but reckon it occurred in the latter half of 1953.

My wife and I were still living with her mother in the family home at 179 Black Road. By this time I had five years service to my name at Barracks Fabrics and had become, I believe, a useful member of the designing team as a colour-separation artist. I recall that just at that time our department had not seen anything of Mr Hermon for some weeks and I had surmised he was probably in London or Paris where he bought many designs; and then I heard, quite casually, that in fact he wasn't too well and was resting at his home.

The particular day I write of had no special feature other than to say that life at Barracks was for me a constantly satisfying challenge, with no two days ever being the same.

How Dorothy and I occupied ourselves that evening I cannot say but as we prepared for bed I felt a sense of unease and as I lay down the feeling intensified within minutes; a deep foreboding, the like of which I'd never experienced before. I sat up and said, *"There's something wrong at Barracks!"*

"Why d'you say that now?" Dorothy asked, *"you've not mentioned it before."* I explained I'd only just got the feeling that something was amiss. *"It's such a strong feeling, as if the firm's on fire or something. D'you think I should go to Saville Street telephone kiosk and phone Mr Jones? Maybe the two of us could go down in his car and check the place over."*

"What, at 11 o'clock at night and just because you're getting funny thoughts in your mind. They're more likely to send men in white coats to take you away! If there's a fire at Barracks it'll soon show itself, without you worrying about it. For goodness sake get to sleep."

But for the most part sleep eluded me that night and, whilst I felt somewhat jaded in the morning, I was in a more relaxed frame of mind and resolved not to discuss my previous night's concern with any of my colleagues.

I could see nothing amiss when I got to work. There had certainly been no fire but I immediately told myself I'd had the foreboding of a crisis, which could have been anything including a fire.

Tom and Annie Hunter (Geoffrey's father and mother) in the back garden of their Hurdsfield home in 1953.

After half an hour's normal working it appeared that my fears had had no substance at all and I was left with only an enigma to ponder... and then, just at that point a girl came in from the office. *"We've just received news that Mr Hermon passed away last night. He died of cancer. I'm sorry to bring you such sad news."*

I believe that story clearly illustrates that Mr Hermon and I had established a special bond and with the severance of that bond, life at Barracks was never quite the same for me again.

In mid-April, 1954, I entered my name on a form at the Beehive public house, Black Road, paid the necessary fee and thereby was registered to compete in an Individual Darts Competition.

I was a somewhat unpredictable darts performer in playing 'round the board', as it was called. I could generally play well up to the point when I was required to hit the bull's-eye in the centre of the board and then chance rather than skill took over. Thirty or forty attempts to hit the bull's-eye was usual. The reason I explain my indifferent play is to make the point that whether I won or not mattered little to me, I was happy to be an occasional participant.

Two weeks later on the sports pages of the Macclesfield Times the first round pairings were published and I saw that I was to attend the Waters Green Tavern before 9pm on Wednesday 4th May, to play Norman Hill of the Star Inn, London Road. Our pairing was just one of several games to be played there that evening and many other town pubs were hosting similar events on the night.

I arrived in good time and when throwing commenced Norman and I were drawn to compete the second game and by 9.15 we stepped up to the oche to throw a few practice darts and then we were off.

The first of the best-of-three legs I raced quickly to the bull and hit the centre without a great deal of difficulty, which was good for my confidence and it seemed I had a reasonable chance of winning.

In the second leg the strangest thing happened. I suffered from what I can only describe as a complete loss of co-ordination. I began to throw my darts as if they were twisted pieces of metal devoid of all aerodynamic potential. It was totally inexplicable and acutely embarrassing to me, for the audience had witnessed within just a few minutes a fairly competent display of darts degenerate to a farcical display of incompetence. Norman took those remaining two legs without being threatened and as we shook hands he asked, *"What the devil happened to you after that first leg? I've never seen anything like it."* *"Nor I,"* I replied. *"I could do nothing about it. I feel as though I've disgraced myself and I've no wish to hang about here."* So home I went puzzled by an experience I'd never had before but determined not to dwell on it. For that reason I didn't say anything more than *"I lost,"* when I arrived home.

I got to work early next morning. When I arrived Bill Dent, the police inspector's son was the only member of staff to have got there before me. I seated myself at my desk, running my eye over my current job to assess my starting point for the new day's labour. I noticed Bill approaching out of the corner of my eye. He spoke quietly, *"I didn't expect to see you this morning, Geoff."* I thought, that's an odd thing to say, and replied, *"Why ever not, Bill?"* He raised his right hand to the level of my desk. It contained a copy of the News Chronicle and he opened it out, front page uppermost, and his finger pointed to a photograph of a wrecked motor car. *"I'm sorry, Geoff, but you're going to have to read that."*

The report under the photograph was of a head-on collision the previous evening which had resulted in two fatalities. One was a man from Lostock Gralam. Suddenly the second name seemed to leap from the page with searing intensity: Thomas Hunter, Crew Avenue, Macclesfield. My father! It was a stunning revelation that rendered me incapable of reading further. I said something like, *"I must go to Mother,"* and in stunned confusion took my coat from the hook and walked out, with a feeling of great physical weakness and made my way the quarter mile to the family home, with a fitful walking-trot, a home that was now filled with sorrow and disbelief.

There were questions to be asked but by now I was in a state of mute acceptance. Dad had gone and no amount of questions and answers would bring him back. In my reticent state I simply listened to others and the story I gleaned was this: A group of pals, all mature men, which included my eldest brother Tony, but not my father, had arranged to go to Chester races that Wednesday, 4th May. I think the group numbered four, and they went by car. Dad went to Chester on the same day, perhaps as a bookies clerk or purely for a day of pleasure.

Late in the day, as the foursome was preparing to leave Chester they met up with Dad and offered to give him a lift home, and he occupied the passenger seat next to the driver with the remaining three in the back. On the way home at a point where the very wide road passes The Smoker public house at Plumley, the Macclesfield car veered to the right and collided head-on with a car containing a husband and wife, with the results as stated. Tony was able to comfort Dad for the few minutes of life left to him.

So, after all, we had something to be thankful for, that Tony and the other lives had been spared. There were injuries, but nothing life-threatening and the police investigation found no reason to take the matter further.

On the evening of the day I learned of the tragedy, May 5th, 1954, Roger Bannister ran the first sub-four minute mile at Oxford, a feat that Dad, had he not missed it by one day, would have enthused over with me. A day later, my youngest brother, Terry had his fifteenth birthday, poor lad.

Yes, Florrie Wright, the greengrocer who employed me in the late 1930s certainly had a point...

7

Hello, Cotton Street!

During the fifties I lived in Cotton Street, Macclesfield, first at number 26 and later at number 28 which was the last house at the bottom of the street close to the top of the Dams Steps.

Both of the houses I lived in, and probably all the houses in that row, were oddly-built structures in that the ground fell so sharply at the rear that to reach their backyard, dwellers had to first go down into their cellars at the back of the house to reach the back door.

Of the two homes my wife and I had number 28 was my favourite. Although very old it was probably the most spacious house in the street being three up, three down, plus the cellars and was a godsend to a young couple with a young son and barely two ha'pennies to rub together. Each house, in its turn, came to us courtesy of Miss Dorothy Casey, headmistress of St. Peter's School, Windmill Street, who, if not exactly the owner of the properties, acted as the agent. Miss Casey, I recall, was a trusting lady, never in a hurry to collect rents. Methodically each week we would place the required sum in a place of safety and whenever the total reached an embarrassing point I would visit her at Larkhall and straighten our account.

When we first arrived in the street in the autumn of 1954 we considered number 26 would benefit from some decorating of which I had no experience at all. The prospect of hanging wallpaper I considered absolutely frightening but I was re-assured by my wife's uncle, Jack Mellor of Gunco Lane, who declared the art *"dead easy"*, but the real breakthrough came from a newspaper advertisement to which I responded and received *Home Decoration and Repairs*, 10/6 from Odhams Press. It was a 'gem' of a publication, superbly illustrated, and today, 50 years later, it reposes in the same cardboard box it arrived in.

I converted an old bedroom screen of Mother's into a pasting board, bought cheap bundles of wallpaper, some as cheap as fourteen pence a roll - slightly less than 6p in today's currency - from Wallpaper Stores Ltd, 81 Mill Street. These were the days when the selvedge had to be trimmed off both sides of each roll and the trade adhesive was boiling water paste.

Can you picture the scene when I started? The cut length of paper was stretched along my pasting board, my pasting brush was 'loaded' and just beyond, propped up on the sideboard and open on the appropriate page was my new Odhams book! Given that I also wore an apron - an absolute 'must' for a paper-hanger - I must have looked like a young wife trying out a recipe!

In fact, that first length of wallpaper I pasted, which was intended for the ceiling of the living room above our front window ended up a hopeless mess on the floor. It was so reminiscent of Laurel and Hardy I had to laugh. and I learnt and progressed from that point on, but more about that later.

Although my work at Barracks Fabrics was fulfilling in an artistic sense the remuneration was such that there was a constant problem coaxing our budget to stretch from one pay day to the next. I remember with affection trotting down the Dams Steps to Gorton and Wilson, builders, for the occasional purchase of cement to mix with accumulated coal-dust for the making of fire-bricketts. Genial Charlie Mitchell, in charge there, would ask only a modest sum each time and Dorothy Barlow, the girl in the office, would acknowledge payment.

Cotton Street was a happy street with a sense of good fellowship prevailing most of the time. Families which come to mind were the Geoghegans, Maddens, Ridgeways, Pimblotts, Cawleys, Grattons, Dales, Suttons (Jim was an old Macclesfield Town FC player) and the Oldfields.

In due course my wife obtained evening employment and I would take

The Dams Steps today. What was the access to the lower end of Barker Street and Cotton Street in the 1950s now has the busy Churchill Way beyond a barrier

over the care of young Paul after completing each day's stint at Barracks.

Each evening, Monday to Friday, Dorothy would take Paul to her friend, Lily Challinor, 23 Duke Street at 5.40 and go to her job at a ribbon factory between Saville Street and Copper Street on Macclesfield Common. I would collect him at 6 o'clock. All very convenient, especially as our homes were so near to each other. Dorothy would return home at 10.20pm.

This was a great bonding period for Paul and me and I made a point, most evenings, of leisurely strolling round the area with him before putting him to bed. In my book, *Waterloo Boy* I told a story of the kindness of the Cass family who owned the Regal Picture House in Duke Street. I repeat the tale here, and make no apology for doing so, because now is the right time for it to be accorded its correct chronological place:

My son Paul was a two-year-old and on his evening walks, prior to bedtime, we would call at the Regal about 7.30 for a chat with Mrs Cass at her pay-box in the sloped open-ended entrance to her cinema. Paul loved to be lifted up to see and to chat with *'the lady in the window'* and he and Mrs Cass developed a great affection for each other.

One evening while thus engaged there was a movement to my left and a glance confirmed that an elderly man had entered the enclosed area from the street. Instinctively, I backed away from the window, Paul in my arms, to allow the newcomer to purchase his ticket. Unexpectedly, the man bent down into a crouched position and shuffled behind me as fast as his old legs would permit, before passing through the swing doors into the cinema.

A smiling Mrs Cass, who had seen everything, responded to the puzzlement in my face. *"Just a poor pensioner,"* she explained. *"He's been coming here for quite some time now. Never misses a programme and always comes half way through the first house. He brings a bit of a tea card or cigarette packet cut to shape. The usherette is instructed to accept his token without comment and to treat it in the normal way. She returns half of it to him and shows him to his seat. It would be cruel to spoil his bit of pleasure, wouldn't it?"*.

I am sure readers will agree that a heartening little tale like that makes for better reading than 'politically correct' decisions which have soured the news in more recent times.

Having put Paul to bed I was far from being bored. My hobby was competitions. I had on order each week the Competitor's Journal which contained all the major newspaper contests and entry forms: John Bull magazine *Bullets*, *News of the World* and *People* crosswords, *Empire News*, Spot the Ball etc, plus the journal's own weekly contests for small money prizes.

John Bull *Bullets* was for me the most satisfying contest of them all. Contestants selected an 'example' from a given list of short terms. The skill lay in adding a further comment of two, three or four words as cleverly as possible. Entry fee was sixpence per Bullet submitted.

Topical issues were the key to success and the wise competitor kept his eye on the calendar, as a full month would pass between entering the Bullets and the publication of the winning names and entries. One prize winning Bullet often recalled to this day was where the competitor chose the term 'For Services Rendered' from the list of examples. For his Bullet he wrote: King, 'pinned on cross'. This has a clever double meaning with the image of a monarch awarding a medal for valour, on the one hand, and a much more powerful comment on our Lord's crucifixion. Now imagine that Bullet being published during Easter week and you have full, prize-winning impact.

In those days, too, competitions abounded in the stores and on the packs of food on their shelves. Commercial radio also played its part. Like so many other local families we subscribed to Mr Parker's Radio Relay. For half-a-crown per week we had four-programme radio on tap and more often than not this included Radio Luxemburg, a truly entertaining service and a boon to competition lovers, particularly on Sunday evenings as I was to find to my profit. It was, you might say, just down my Cotton Street!

Although through the years, my Bullets successes were meagre, it was an apprenticeship of tremendous value in the use of word-play and has steered me to many a success in the years since.

RELY on RELAY!

Perfectly Simple **Simply Perfect**

8

A Change of House

I reckon our stay in 26 Cotton Street lasted about a year. Having no inkling that number 28 would eventually become available I had decorated - painted and papered - throughout the house, thanks to my wife's willingness to invest some of her hard-earned evening wages in this cosmetic exercise. In that first year, I remember, I had bought a second-hand ladder from my window-cleaner, Alban Burgess, and beautified the exterior wood of number 26 a rich maroon, having obtained permission from Miss Casey to do so.

At this point the Oldfields at 28 announced they would shortly be leaving our street for Leigh Street and, being good tenant neighbours, advised us to contact Miss Casey promptly should we wish to change houses. This we did and Miss Casey was happy to agree, asking for an increase in our weekly rent from something like 9/3d to 10/6d. This switch of homes was ideal in more ways than one. We didn't need to order a big van, for one thing! But the big bonus for me was that I now had two downstairs rooms looking

Cotton Street, courtesy of Macclesfield Borough Council.
These two photographs, combined, show all 14 of the houses on Geoffrey's side of the
street. At the bottom of the hill the Dams steps descended to the left.
In the bottom photo, the photographer had his back to Edgar Freeman's grocer shop.

Sporting life at Barracks Fabrics 1960s.
L to R: Frank Lovatt, Geoff Burrows, Tom Bentley & Geoff Hunter

out on to the street, one to be used as a living room and one as a working den for my various activities.

At that particular time I was Results Secretary for Macclesfield Table Tennis Association, with Monday evenings a regular working night bringing the league tables up-to-date following the previous week's matches and sending reports to Ernest Hackney ('Top Spin') of the Macclesfield Times. The relationship with Ernie was one I treasured right up to his death many years later.

It meant my charts could now be stuck on the walls of my den and not rolled up at the evening's end. And there was my art work. I could now leave a cartoon half-finished and return to it the next night, for since my demob my cartoons had appeared in the two Manchester evening papers, the News and Chronicle, locally in the Courier and Times, The Sunday Pictorial, The Athletic Review and fairly regularly in Competitor's Journal.

To have a den where I could abandon a piece of art-work and recommence a day or so later was absolute bliss!

Naturally my wife wanted our 'new' home to be decorated to her taste, so I set to again, progressively moving from the downstairs rooms, which had a greater priority in Dorothy's strategy, before commencing my assault on the bedrooms. The living room was decorated by me throughout the night, commencing at 11pm on the Friday and working till 8am on Saturday. This worked so well I have done it on several occasions through the years.

In those early decorating years, learning as I went along, I had a strong point in my favour. Textile design was my trade and I spotted immediately that wallpaper design had a similar variant repeat behaviour to what I was used to, and I could quickly ascertain how to rotate the rolls of paper to limit wastage. Also, I was fastidious in ensuring accurate repeating ('matching up' in other words) particularly over and under windows.

In due course the strangest thing happened; people started knocking at my door inviting me to decorate for them.

The first caller was Mrs Sutton at number 18: she wanted a change of bedroom decor and could I tell her how many rolls of paper to buy? Before visiting her house I had to think about charges... decorating for others was a new experience for me.

After a little thought I called on her, quickly measured the bedroom and said that normally I would charge 50/- and supply my own paste but I would deduct 5/- as she and her husband Jim were pensioners. This figure pleased her and, having assured me that the ceiling and wall paper would be purchased in time I promised to decorate that weekend, Saturday and Sunday.

I had never been in the Sutton's home before and I commented on how attractive were the pieces of lace here and there, that were a feature of the house. *"It's tatting,"* Mrs Sutton explained, *"I do a lot of it."* That claim proved to be a mammoth understatement.

The word 'tatting' was new to me and probably is to many of my readers. This is what my dictionary has to say about it: Tatting 1. An intricate type of lace made by looping a thread of cotton or linen by means of a hand shuttle. 2. The act or work of producing this.

Having expressed an inquisitive admiration for the samples of her work on view and been shown the small shuttle, allied to her own dexterity that could produce so complex a lace, I queried the time it must have taken to produce just a few square inches.

"These pieces are nothing compared to my bigger items," she said,

"I'll show you." And from out of drawers and cupboards she produced large tablecloths, bedspreads and suchlike: an abundance I would have thought impossible for one person to produce in their lifetime, with just a

simple thread and a little gadget held between her fingers.

I often wonder what became of those lace masterpieces...

So decorating the Sutton's bedroom (and their landing a fortnight later) was the start of my being employed weekends, on average about every 6 weeks, and always unsolicited. It helped to pay the coal bills.

9

Rough and Smooth

Following my marriage in 1952 I made a point of visiting my mother every working-day lunchtime after I had dined at Barracks canteen. By the mid to late fifties I was the only one of her off-spring able to offer a bit of mid-day company. My six siblings were all tied up with either marriage, jobs or distance so my close proximity was an important feature of Mother's life, and that 1.15 cuppa we shared was stimulating in more ways than one.

This particular day I write of was unusual in that Mother had a message for me. A woman resident of Arbourhay Street had called on her that morning with a tearful plea for my help as a decorator. Could I call and see her that evening after work?

"It's something to do with her sister visiting her and she can't get a decorator at such short notice. Here's her address." I promised to call that evening, and did.

The lady in question was an elderly spinster *"Can you help, please? My sister is visiting me the weekend of next week. I can't put her in the back bedroom, the state it's in. Follow me and I'll show you."* She continued with her story as we climbed the stairs. *"I asked Howard Barker first."* (His shop was on Commercial Road, one minute's walk from her home) *"Then I tried Barker's in Cumberland Street, followed by George Bennett in Mill Lane. They all said the same thing - too busy. I'm getting too old for all that traipsing about."* Her back bedroom was surprisingly large. *"I've got the paper, and it must be done this coming weekend."*

"I'll be here 8 o'clock Saturday morning. Who's stripping this old paper off?" I asked.

"Forget about any stripping. Stick the new paper over the top - nobody'll notice."

"Can't do that, love; that old paper's too loose - you can see that yourself. In fact when that paper comes off these walls will need a good sizing before any fresh paper goes on."

She made a snorting noise, *"Well you'll have to do it."*

"Make that a 7 o'clock start then, Saturday morning." On the way home I remembered I'd not not mentioned the £2-5/- it was going to cost her. I took comfort in the knowledge she had tried in vain to get professional help.

Saturday morning was spent in preparation. The old paper came off fairly easily, helped by a little hot water at times; then a good sanding-down followed by a glue-size coat, ceiling and walls. The room, incidentally, was bare apart from the two old chairs that supported my plank. The afternoon was spent papering the ceiling and adding the frieze and at tea-time I left for home promising to be back at nine the next morning.

The Sunday work went well but predictably slowly and by the time the border had been applied it was close to 8pm. Washing my bucket and brushes at her kitchen sink downstairs she said, *"I suppose it's getting time for you to be paid?"* To which I replied it was the custom to settle-up immediately the job was completed. *"Will 30/- be enough?"* she asked.

"No, it will not," I replied. *"My fee is 45/-. I'm not charging you for stripping the walls and I've supplied the glue-size and paste. You'd have been charged a lot more had Barker's done it."*

"Yes, that may be so, but you're only an amateur."

"That is perfectly true," I countered, *"but I only charge amateur prices."*

"Well, I'm prepared to increase my offer to 35/- and not a penny more. Take it or leave it."

"I'll take it," I said and held out my hand, and having received the money, I said *"The next time you have a decorating crisis don't bother my mother with your problem. There'll be no way she can help."*

That Sunday wasn't my day at all. I'd also missed my competition half-hour on Radio Luxemburg. It was ending as I arrived back home.

In stark contrast to that disappointing tale this second story unfolded a few weeks later.

One evening I'd called as usual at Lily Challinor's Duke Street home to collect Paul on my way home from work. Lily informed me that her aunt in Crompton Road would like to see me about decorating her front room. I called on her aunt that weekend to find she and her husband were quite elderly. The

front room was already stripped with the rolls of ceiling and wallpaper in a
tidy bundle by the wall.

"How quick can you decorate this room?" the lady asked.

"I can do it next Saturday and Sunday but I can't promise what time I'll
finish. I like to take my time." It was better than admitting I was a slow worker.

"What will it cost?" The lady again. "Well, since you're pensioners, it'll
cost you £2-5/-." A quick glance of tacit understanding passed between them
and with the intention of relieving them of any mutual discomfort they shared,
I said hurriedly, "Look, if money's tight I'm quite prepared to knock off the five
bob if that'll help."

At that the husband spoke for the first time. "Lad, if tha does as tha sez,
next weekend, whatever time tha finishes, there'll be a fiver on that table fer
thee!" His wife added her own rider to his assurance. "My first husband was
a decorator and I know the cost of things."

I must have pleased them that weekend. They had me back two weeks
later to decorate their living room. On the same terms, of course.

10
A Friendship Delayed

As one would expect, the workforce at Barracks Fabrics was predominately
male. Only at the office end - the first part of the extensive factory as one
entered Lower Heys gate - was there something like a balanced gender,
mainly because that section contained the designing room with work
common to both sexes.

I have already mentioned May Hirst and Dorothy Harris (a jewellers
daughter from Congleton). Other names I recall with warmth during the
fifties and early sixties are Kathy Whiston, a young married lady, Freda
Moss, Wendy Harrison, who, like Les Anderton, lived out of town, Vivian
Dale, Sheila Ward, Jill Hadfield and Joyce Sweeney. Not surprisingly
wedding bells chimed almost every year and surnames changed accordingly.

What a talented bevy of ladies they were, artists every one. It is fair to
say the success of the whole designing room team owed much to the room's
manager, Mr Jones, who controlled his staff with the wisdom of Solomon,
and did so for many future years.

There was one little lady - she was less than five feet in height - whom I considered something of a mystery. She was a designer who worked apart from the rest of us, in her own work-room along the corridor. So far as I could judge, she didn't liaise with our department either and, strange as it may seem, it would be forty years before I got to know her as a true friend!

Edith Buxton will be a name known by many in Macclesfield today for her brilliant watercolour floral paintings, the exhibitions at her charming cottage in Blakelow Road and using her skill to benefit numerous charities. Based on the many chats we had about the past I am able to say that she enjoyed an exalted position as a designer at Barracks and her own small studio was a status symbol of her standing. Whenever Mr Hermon and a small attendant group visited London or Paris in search of new designs, Edith was always one of their number and, interestingly, she was always booked into a different hotel from the all male party. Propriety was a word much more in vogue then, than it is today.

Edith Buxton working at her easel during her retirement

Most children born in Macclesfield early in the 1900s could be said to have had a humble beginning and Edith was no exception. Here is a letter, typical of her style, which I received in 1993, undated, unaddressed, and without a traditional introduction, or closure. She knew she could take such liberties with her friends.

Marion has brought for me to read your Waterloo Sunset and therein is the whole of my early childhood, from my birth in Gas Row, 1908. Commercial Road, Arbourhay Street, Daybrook Street and Waterloo Street were my world. I attended Daybrook Street School from infancy and Fence Sunday School.

Commercial Road was a complete and perfect shopping 'mall'; there your every need could be satisfied and they were all your friends, too. Remember the cloggers? There I sat waiting for my clogs to be fitted with new irons, fourpence, before I went to school. My paternal grandmother lived in what I remember as the Gas Yard and my aunt and uncle in Waterloo Street. Claytons, three cousins, Tom, Jack and Nellie; we all went to that haven for children, Fence Sunday School. What teachers! Grimshaws, Leahs, Kirkhams; names that deserve pure gold letters for their service to the children of that area.

Concerts for which we had practice nights and we, too, had a Band of Hope. We also had another wonderful teacher, Alice Pyatt, who then lived at the top of the 108 steps, who came to teach us club-swinging. We travelled as far as the YMCA in Manchester with Alice to swing clubs, a splendid enterprise and adventure. I doubt we had ever been on a train before. I particularly remember the YMCA for the firemens' poles we had to use between floors. Whatever else I do badly or otherwise, I breathe well because of Alice Pyatt and now, nearing 85, the hills of Blakelow are to me as the flat is to my contemporaries. Shutlingslow would still present no problem.

Bicycles and tennis, for example, were luxuries unknown to us, so for children of the Fence Sunday School Alice was yet one more of their angels.

Clara Kirkham took us for a walk through Bollington fields and we had to find a four leaf clover, and afterwards to her home for a lovely tea.

We played by the Bollin and the only dolls we knew were made from the clay from Bollinside and baked in the oven. We played safely in the woods that were on our doorstep. Davenport's delivered milk night and morning by the horse and float - it was a wonderful area when one thinks of it now and brings to mind all the shops from end to end of Commercial Road, even to Arighi's who were just as wonderful as they are now. We didn't run around looking for 'discounts'; we trusted and rightly so. Poor as we were, everything came from Arighi's.

You must have been overwhelmed with correspondence from we who live in Macclesfield, Geoffrey. I am remembering a couple of decades earlier than you and have, in my mind, now demolished the present Commercial Road and rebuilt it just as it was, perfect for contented living.

We became a one parent family and at 12 I went to work to offer a little support. The half-timers were the income-support in those days and we no longer lived in the Gas Row. I went to work at 6.30am.

From the period of life, 8 years old to my marriage to Joe Buxton in 1930, life was pure hell. Normally, I think if one has known nothing different then it matters not, or perhaps not quite so much, but I have always had an awareness, a sensitivity, and I was deeply scarred.

When I married, my first home was No 12 Steeple Street and I was back to shop in Hurdsfield. Mr Kirk's, Palin's, Longshaw's, Clark's, Bainbridge's, Sally Wilkinson of the fruit shop, who filled any size bag for sixpence, well assorted. Then, in 1930, it hadn't changed to the horror it is now and my father-in-law, Joe Buxton, kept the Woodman Inn and there I met your parents and got to know them well. You lived on the estate where in my childhood I had gathered bluebells in the woods of Davenport's farm. There was no estate then.

These, of course, are just notes as I remember....

Gas Row was the short row of terraced cottages of Hurdsfield Road, on the left as it terminated approaching the Gas Road/Hibel Road junction (since demolished). Just as Thorpe Street was known as Clock Alley in the same area, Gas Row was another example of Victorian dubbing.

Edith and I 'found' each other again in the late 1980s and from that point on I was a constant visitor to her home, particularly enjoying her coffee mornings with a cluster of other friends.

She died on February 2, 1996 aged 87.

11
'Tick'

Way back in the 1950s a small area had been cleared behind the Majestic in Duke Street for the parked cars of that cinema's patrons, but what a difference there is to that area now! A vast expanse of space given to parking - at a cost - with scarcely a hint of the homes of the generations of dwellers who contributed so much to our town's proud working history.

From Roe Street's lower side, Silk Street, Charles Street, Barker Street and Cotton Street, for which I had so much affection, have gone without trace and only Duke Street with little more than half remaining, hangs on to its identity.

Yes, it was an old part of town and although a few houses in Barker Street could claim a nearness to modernity, the feeling I had for the area was that most families, including my own, had income in sympathy with their accommodation, and each cheerfully accepted the fact.

"We've nowt to spare!" might well have been a unanimous lament, but such was the camaraderie, it could have been a battle cry of unity.

It's no wonder that credit (or 'tick' as it was more often called), played so big a part in the lives of those around us then. I'm not thinking of hire-purchase which, entered into prudently, was a boon to the working class at that time. No, I'm thinking of the weekly grocery bill. The 'little shops' used to allow 'tick' throughout the week and the customer 'settled up' on a Friday evening or Saturday morning, usually, then the credit cycle started all over again. Wages were paid on Friday in those days. Mind you, if a person had ready cash and the time to shop around, savings could be made shopping in the Market Place and Mill Street.

Main shops at that time were Seymour Mead, Redman's (my favourite, due to its fresh, bright ambience), Home and Colonial and N.& G. Burden's, either side of Gallimore's barber shop, Hunter's Stores, the Maypole Dairy, Burgon's, George Mason and F. & E. Taylor next to the White Lion Hotel. Also handy was M.E.P.S. (Co-op) at 32 Roe Street.

The two grocers who served the rectangle of life in which I lived were Edgar Freeman of Silk Street who was married to a sister of the Woodward brothers of Brocklehurst Avenue, and J.C.Leigh of Roe Street, on the corner of Prospect Buildings.

My wife preferred doing business with Mr Leigh, even though his shop was further away from our home. No doubt Dorothy had her reasons.

The trouble with 'tick' was that once you'd settled up at the weekend, all too often there was little coinage left to play with and by Monday that little bit had dissipated with Sunday purchases made elsewhere. This could lead to mini crises and embarrassment, and a particular story comes to mind concerning a mother who lived close by who was sufficiently streetwise to impress me with her guile.

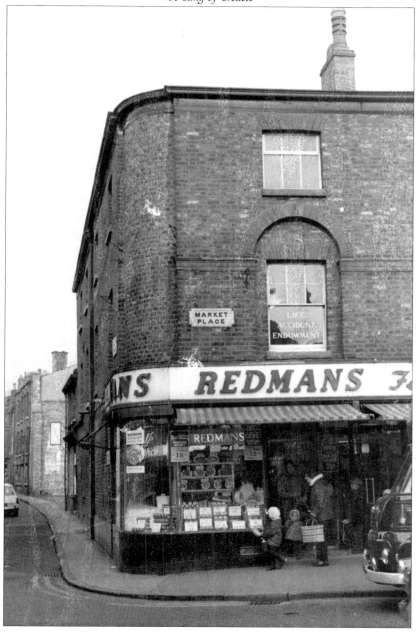

Redman's.

It was around 3.30 one Thursday afternoon, Dorothy was returning from a walk with Paul who was aged 3 at the time. She was called from an open doorway and invited in for a cup of tea. A little boy of Paul's age was playing on the rug and the mother explained that her other two children, a girl of 8 and a boy of 6 would be arriving home from school shortly, which they did.

Immediately on entering her home the girl announced that on the morrow she had to take a shilling for the school photograph. The mother opened the top drawer in her sideboard and withdrew a small red notebook and handing it to the girl said, *"Take the book to Mr Freeman and tell him your mum wants a siphon of soda water. Don't forget to say 'please' - and no running with the siphon when you've got it; we don't want any accidents."*

A few minutes later the girl arrived back from her errand, the siphon hugged to her chest, the notebook stuck down the front of her dress. She was relieved of her burden, patted on the head for a job well done and told to take a seat at the table, and the other children, including Paul, were asked to do the same. Then the mother went to a cupboard for four cups which she lined up on the table and half-filled each from the siphon, passing the cups to each child before returning her attention to Dorothy and their earlier conversation.

Over the next half-hour or so, with further half-filled cups of soda water issued when necessary, the siphon was emptied and the girl was called upon again to return the much lighter siphon to Mr Freeman's shop. It is worth pointing out at this stage that the cost of a full siphon was 4/6d: 1/6d for the soda water plus a 3/- deposit for the siphon.

Shortly afterwards the girl returned and placing 3/- on the table (as luck would have it, a florin and a shilling) she said, *"Mr Freeman's sent you that, Mum"*. The mother handed her daughter the shilling. *"That's for your school photograph, tomorrow"* she said casually, as she placed the florin in her purse.

I salute that mother. It would have been so easy and convenient to send her daughter to school with a white lie on her lips that Friday morning, (*"Please, Miss, I've forgotten to bring my shilling, But I'll bring it on Monday"*) but the mother was having none of that! Her girl had been told to bring a shilling to school that Friday morning, and she would toe the line with the best of her classmates. And she did.

12
My Prize Collection

In February, 1957, our daughter, Lorraine was born to add to our joy and I was, at this point, enjoying a fair degree of success, competition-wise with Radio Luxemburg to the extent that I was dubbed *The Count of Luxemburg* by my friends. Sunday evenings seemed to be most lucky for me. Competitions were launched, judged and winners announced on a weekly basis so speed off the mark was crucial.

Mostly they were 'postcard' comps but, to my delight, not 'first out of the hat' contests. A popular clause in the rules was, 'State your answer on a postcard in as entertaining a way as possible', and if the postcard wasn't mentioned then ingenuity knew no bounds.

Coincidence played its part in the story of a success I have been leading up to. In the spring of 1957 some wag at Barracks Fabrics came to my table in the canteen one lunchtime and, seating himself opposite me, placed before me a small rectangular piece of thin frosted perspex set in a wooden base. I was asked to keep my eye on this small white screen standing up in front of me. He then struck a match and passed the flame from side to side across the back of the perspex.

To my surprise the lighted match revealed a silhouette scene of two figures, one apparently moving. It was a vulgar presentation which I do not wish to say any more about, but if I was not impressed by the idea's crude application, I most certainly was by its conception.

Why had the moving flame created a moving image, I wanted to know. The reason, it transpired, was simple. One of the silhouette figures had been painted directly on to the back of the perspex, the other had been cut out of black card and stuck slightly away from the perspex surface and it was this figure's shadow changing with the movement of the flame which gave the illusion of movement.

I might well have forgotten that incident had not Currys, the leading bicycle dealers at that time, sponsored The Winifred Atwell Show on Luxemburg each Sunday evening and two weeks later supplied a competition format I could not ignore. During the programme Miss Atwell played a snatch of a popular song on her piano for that week's competition and listeners were asked to identify the song and let Currys know, in as entertaining a way as possible, the song's title. Entries had to be received by Thursday and the winner of a bicycle would be announced the following Sunday. A postcard was not mentioned.

The song's title was *By the Light of the Silvery Moon* and the shadow idea immediately came to mind. I purchased a box of Swan Vestas and over the next two nights papered the box with fine art paper, adapted the tray to incorporate a screen of thick tracing paper behind which was painted the silhouette of a young miss sitting on a park bench with a crescent moon above. The girl's face, profiled with puckered lips, faced her beau. He, I had carefully cut out of a black card and secured with glue into the correct position, his face facing hers. Tests with a moving flame confirmed that his body moved towards her each time and his kisses were perfectly placed. The sleeve of the box was colourfully decorated with the title, Pocket Telly presents *By the Light of the Silvery Moon* (see back of box for instructions).

The complete unit was packed in a flat toffee tin and posted to London on Wednesday lunchtime. Sure enough on Sunday evening I was announced the winner and, later, Currys wrote with their congratulations and offered me a choice of their Congleton or Buxton store for the presentation. I opted for Buxton and the Friday afternoon of Barnaby Week was mutually agreed.

Mother, whom I visited daily, asked, *"Have you got anything to go in?"* I replied that I'd got a decent blazer and trousers for starters. *"I'll buy you a new shirt"*, she said, and was as good as her word. Shoe-wise I was a bit tatty but this problem was to be solved.

Daily papers early that Barnaby Week carried details of the escape of convicts from Wakefield Prison but news that mattered to me was contained in Competitor's Journal announcing I had won a cartoon contest and £2 was on its way to me. The shoe problem was solved.

Come Friday, then, I caught the bus to Buxton, delighted with my attire and confident that mother could have no complaints about my appearance. I arrived at Currys store, Spring Gardens, at 3pm and was greeted by the manager, a smiling, dapper gent whose name does not readily come to mind.

"We've plenty of time", he said. *"The photographer's not due until 4.30. First, come and inspect the cycles and take your pick, then I can put a 'SOLD' ticket on it"*. So back and forth we went, he commenting on the merits of each.

I was not interested in anything racy and chose a more traditional model, red and silver in colour, with three-speed and hub-lighting, and expressed a desire to ride it home once the presentation and publicity had been completed.

In the meantime the two of us adjourned for coffee to the Barbecue Restaurant, 100 yards up the road nearer to the Pavilion Gardens. Coffee followed coffee during which he and I exchanged career and family stories and, inevitably, discussed competitions. We returned to the store in glorious sunshine. I answered reporters' questions and posed for photographs holding the cycle.

At 4.45 the sky darkened dramatically outside and it began to rain steadily. *"You can't ride home in that"*, said the manager. *"Not to worry, I'll get the van to deliver it, Monday or Tuesday. You'll have to catch the bus back I'm afraid"*.

I thanked all present for their kindness, left the store and crossed to the other side of Spring Gardens where the shop blinds would offer better protection as I moved towards the bus stop. I reached the Barbecue again and paused, first checking my watch and then looking into the window pondering whether to have a final coffee before my time of departure.

It was then I felt a firm hand on my shoulder. The sort of act which adds further pressure to a guilty conscience. I turned without such trepidation to find a police officer confronting me. Not only that, a police car had slid silently into the kerb during my brief spell of contemplation. *"Mind telling me your name?"* asked the bobby. I said, *"Look its raining. Mind if I shelter in your car - I'm getting wet through!"* He seemed to be rather taken aback by this and then gestured me to sit alongside the driver. He climbed into the back and returned to his role of questioner.

I told him who I was and where I was from. Suddenly, he reached down between my back and the back of the seat and appeared to remove a dirty folded newspaper. *"What's this?"* he asked and then answered the question himself. *"Oh, it's only your newspaper"*. I bristled at that. *"I beg your pardon"*, I cried indignantly. *"That newspaper has no connection with me. If you think I'd carry a filthy thing like that around with me then you're very much mistaken"*.

"What are you doing here in Buxton?" So I told them the story of my prize presentation. *"Look"*, I pointed out, *"You've only got to drive a 100*

yards down this road to Currys and the manager will confirm everything".
So we drove to Currys, only to find the premises closed.

It began to look as if it wasn't my lucky day after all. *"I'm sorry, but
I've got just three minutes to catch my bus back to Macclesfield. You'll just
have to excuse me"*. I fumbled for the door catch. Firm pressure was applied
to my shoulder again.

"Stay where you are". said the voice behind me. *"We're taking you for
a ride in the country. There's an old lady we'd like you to meet. Everything
will depend on whether she can identify you or not."*

And off we drove. I hadn't a clue where I was being taken nor was I
unduly concerned about it. There was, I felt, a comedy-script scenario about
the whole thing. Several minutes later we drove up to and parked outside a
country cafe, an old stone building. An old lady framed in the open doorway
must be the lady in question, I surmised, so I quickly let myself out of the car
and approached her with the bobby hurriedly following me.

"See here, missus", I said, doing my best to introduce a flavour of good
humour into my performance, *"D'ya mind telling me what's going on? What
sort of hospitality is it Buxton offers when a decent bloke like me can't come
and spend a quiet afternoon minding his own business without being roped
in by your police force?"*

The old lady glance at the bobby and shook her head wearily from side
to side. *"This isn't him, officer"* she confirmed. *"The other fella hadn't
anything like as much to say as this one!"* The officer turned to me and
spread out his arms. *"That's the way it goes, but we had to be sure before
allowing you to go. Sorry to have troubled you. I hope that new bike of yours
gives you many happy years of cycling. So long."* And with that he settled
himself in the front seat next to the driver.

"Whoa, whoa there", I wasn't having this. *"You can't leave me here.
You've brought me into the middle of nowhere. The very least you can do is to
drop me off where you picked me up, right?"* *"Right"*, said the man. On the
way back to the town he explained the situation. Earlier that day a suspicious-
looking man had spent rather a long time in the old lady's cafe and she had
become increasingly uneasy about his presence. When, finally he had gone on
his way she cleared his table and discovered that the dirty folded newspaper he
had left behind was a Wakefield publication. Aware of the recent prison escape
she had called the police and the description she gave them matched my own.

Barnaby Week - Macclesfield holidaymakers line up for the train at Central Station.

'Puffing Billy' at Hibel Road.

From this point on the story free-wheels to a happy conclusion. I arrived home later than planned with an extra story to tell and the cycle was delivered to me the following Tuesday. I've often wondered - since chance decreed my attire was inappropriate for a visit to Buxton that particular day, would a loose, light-coloured suit with large arrow motifs have been less conspicuous?

13

World Premiere

In the spring of 1958 I returned home from work one Thursday evening to find an old copy of Readers' Digest on the sideboard, Dorothy having returned home with it from a visit to friends. Dorothy had ceased work since Lorraine's birth the year before and I could enjoy the luxury of idly browsing through the Digest whilst waiting for tea to be served. I was half-way through the magazine when, on turning one page to the next I was immediately captivated by a superb black and white drawing at the top of the page.

It was of an ocean liner, its bow and part of its hull submerged in water though the vessel was still illuminated by its electrical power. The stern of the ship, its propellers stilled, was high in the air, and close by was a huge iceberg, and here and there tiny lifeboats with people huddled in them; a tragic picture, superbly encapsulated by the artist. After tea, I read the story accompanying the illustration and what an enthralling tale it proved to be.

It was, of course, the story of the Titanic, the largest ship in the world, the luxury liner that struck an iceberg south of Newfoundland on its maiden voyage on the night of April 14-15, 1912 with the loss of 1513 lives. The ship, reputed to be unsinkable due to the water-tight compartments in its hull was carrying lifeboats for less than half its own passengers and crew, these being intended for other imperilled craft lacking the Titanic's guaranteed buoyancy!

I was aged 30 the night I read that story in 1958. Prior to that date I'd known only the barest details from vague, rare references to the ship. The immensity of its loss was never mentioned in my school years and although my parents had always ensured we children kept abreast of current affairs

with newspapers regularly delivered to our home, I cannot ever remember reading any reference to it. I find this puzzling, considering the interest given to the subject since that time.

I was so impressed with the statistics associated with the Titanic story that I acquainted my work colleagues with them during morning tea-break the next day, for example: The ship took 1400 workers 4 years to build. It was a sixth of a mile in length. Over 300 luminaries of all nations had booked first class to savour the opulence on offer. At Southampton, the port of departure, it took on board 650 tons of coal as fuel. At Queenstown, Ireland, which was the final pick-up port for passengers, many of the 100 or so third class (steerage) emigrants had never seen a water closet before boarding Titanic.

When, later that day I completed my work for that week, that should have been the end of the story. I little knew that coincidence had a part to play and, in fact, the story was just beginning.

Two days later, on the Sunday evening, I settled in my chair at 8 o'clock to listen to my favourite Radio Luxemburg half-hour, knowing that it would contain a competition of some sort and a challenge I might be unable to resist. From habit, I felt I had earned this little treat. Earlier that evening I'd put on my coat, left home, descended the Dams Steps and strolled along Elizabeth Street making for Park Lane and Orme's little sweet shop which, by my reckoning now, was number 111. Peanuts for my wife, sweets of one kind or another deemed suitable for Paul, then aged four, and small Cadbury's milk chocolate bars for Lorraine, aged 14 months. Usually I would pause for a chat with the Ormes,a charming young couple, about confectionery promotions and, when available, take contest entry forms home with me. Now I was in my chair, the children had received their ration of sweets and in the background there was a fairly quiet sound of nuts being crunched!

The Luxemburg programme was of general film content with the presenter, Anthony Marriott, a man destined to increase his revenue in later years as co-playwright of the highly successful *No Sex, Please, We're British.*

As usual Mr Marriott kept me waiting that night. It was not until 8.25 that he said, *"And now its competition time. Currently a film is being made at Pinewood Studios of a disaster at sea that shocked the world in April, 1912. What I want to know is the title of the film being made and the name of its director. Here's a clue to the director: he also directed the film The October Man. Send your answers on a postcard to this address... in time for the judging on Thursday. There will be two winners and their names will be announced in next week's programme."* He went on to say what prizes were being offered but I was so stunned by the incredible coincidence of it all I could take in no more.

One thing was very clear to me. Surely, I was meant to enter that contest, and I would.

My Sunday evening experience, allied to my enthusiasm for the Titanic story two days earlier, seemed so incredible to my Barracks colleagues it was a major talking point the next day.

No one could suggest an answer to either of the questions that had been asked. Today, similar type questions to the director query would be simple, thanks to the prolific film-lore research and publications of the late Leslie Halliwell and those who have followed him, but in 1958 such knowledge was confined mainly to those working in the business. I resolved to approach Mr Mellor, manager of the Picturedrome, that evening, following tea.

This proved no difficulty at all; within minutes of asking to see him shortly after seven, I was in his office explaining my quandary.

He slowly shook his head, *"I can't give you any information of any new film dealing with a sea disaster"* he said, *"You could do with talking to a regular 'Picturegoer' reader for that. But if we can find The October Man among the film leaflets on this shelf, and there are hundreds there going back years, we'll name the director you want. Here, you go through that batch and I'll go through these.....*" It took us about twenty minutes to check every leaflet, all to no avail.

"*Sorry about that*" said Mr Mellor. "*Now these few leaflets on this higher shelf are new releases just in,*" he reached up and brought the leaflets down to desk level as he added resigningly, "*so they'll be no use to you.*" As his hand released them and swept across his desk dismissively I was amazed to see the topmost leaflet displayed in full colour, for promotional purposes, an ocean liner sinking beneath the waves, with all the additional detail of the Reader's Digest illustration! I don't recall whether I shouted "*Eureka!*" but we shook hands warmly, enthusing at this sudden resolution of my problem.

The film advertised was *A Night to Remember*, starring Kenneth More, directed by Roy Baker. Mr Mellor bade me "*Good comping*" as I left for home and I considered what tactics to adopt for my postcard entry... By the time I reached home I'd made up my mind.

I remembered that twenty years earlier I had received a free gift one week with my Hotspur boys' paper, tuppence every Friday. In a fairly large envelope I had been given several sheets of waxed paper, with instructions of how it was possible to 'lift-off' a newspaper photograph or a printed item in a newspaper by placing The waxed paper over the the desired area, holding it down firmly and rubbing it with the edge of a coin.

Having peeled the waxed impression from the newspaper it could be transferred to any other paper surface - in a letter one was writing, for instance - by the same coin rubbing process. Far easier to demonstrate than to describe, I might add.

Most importantly, I knew that the inner lining of Kellogg's cornflakes of those days was of the same waxed paper and I intended that evening to transfer the Digest illustration to my postcard, as my entry in the competition. I calculated that on my postcard I could spare less than a quarter inch space top and bottom for my address and answers, and these I had to write in indian ink before the waxed picture was applied.

From arriving home from the Drome to completing my postcard took only ten minutes and within another two minutes it was in the post-box in Elizabeth Street, for collection early next day.

A curious reader might well ask: since the Reader's Digest was an old

The Picturedrome cinema.

copy and likely to be dispensable, why couldn't I stick the original drawing on the postcard? The answer is that you don't win prizes in postcard contests by making it obvious you've conveniently taken a short-cut. My waxed paper dodge, giving the appearance of the sea-tragedy being drawn actually on the postcard itself, implied that I was the artist, although I never claimed to be.

The following Sunday evening - it had been a long week - I, and quite a number of my workmates tuned in to Radio Luxemburg and I was declared one of the two winners, the other being a man from Chester, and a promise to us both that we would get details of our prize within days.

I received my letter on Tuesday of that week: An invitation for me and a companion to attend the World Premiere of *A Night to Remember* on the Friday week, meeting our host, Anthony Marriott at the Rank Organisation H.Q. South Street, London at 3pm.

The arrival of the letter excited me sufficiently to dance a little jig in our front room. *"Missus,"* I declared, *"we're going to London to see a film at the Leicester Square Theatre - the World Premiere, no less!"* Dorothy was quick to dispute me. *"Correction. You are going to London, not me. You and someone else."*

"Ahhh, I know what you're thinking", I countered, *"but you don't need to worry about the children. Your mother will be only too glad to look after them - it's only for one day."*

"You're wrong. It's not the kids I'm worried about. It's myself. How on earth can I go to a big event like that? I've nothing to wear. Come to that, what are you going to wear? You haven't a suit to your name. And who's going to pay your train fare? Seems to me you'd be better entering contests where winning doesn't cost you anything."

I couldn't argue; these were valid points. I said, *"Maybe they'll pay me expenses when I get there."* *"And pigs might fly,"* said Dorothy.

I continued to view my position with sanguine aplomb, convinced that fate had favoured me with a sequence of good-fortune and would continue to do so; and so it proved.

Next morning at tea-break I showed my work colleagues the premiere invitation and reported the conversation I'd had with my wife. Gordon Lennard, who occupied the desk just in front of mine, responded immediately. *"The lack of a suit is no problem. You're the same size as me and I've a spare dark blue suit you can borrow. I'll bring it this afternoon , you can take it home tonight to try on and if it fits, keep it until you're back from London."* Just like that. Wonderful support from a pal and a perfect fit.

On the Friday evening that week as I reached Hurdsfield Road, I met my elder brother Tony who was a tax-man at Hibel Road. He'd heard from Mother most of my story and I filled in the gaps. He said, *"So the Premiere is a week today. I'll make a deal with you. I'll be your companion, I'll pay the rail fare for the pair of us, which currently will be a total of about twenty pounds but if it transpires they pay you expenses you pay me the outlay back. Okay?"* I had no problem with that, thanked Tony and we arranged to meet at Hibel Road station the following Friday just before 11am.

South Street, London W1 runs very close to the Dorchester Hotel. The Rank Organisation premises we were seeking was one of a terrace of large Georgian houses. A pleasing feature for the two of us as we approached the rendezvous was to see a plaque on the wall of one of these fine premises stating that Florence Nightingale had lived there.

We had timed our 3pm arrival perfectly and were greeted warmly by Anthony Marriott. He introduced us to his colleague and the other contest winner from Chester who had brought his girlfriend.

My winning postcard had been given pride of place on the mantelpiece. Predictably, I was asked about its creation and I told them quite truthfully how Kellogg's waxed paper had come to my rescue. Yes, they had thought I was the artist but awarded me full marks for enterprise.

We spent an hour discussing British films, then the six of us left by taxi and were taken the short drive to the Park Lane Hotel for dinner. It was all very grand. The main course was roast duckling served on silver plates and we drank whisky and soda water throughout the meal. Perhaps that accounts for how little I remember. I know we talked and dawdled so long that we finally had to make a hasty dash by taxi for the Leicester Square Theatre.

The crowds.... It was bedlam. The film fans, mainly women, were being kept back by ropes and policemen. It seemed to take us ages to make it into the theatre's foyer where, on the right, a row of elderly ladies sat, perhaps twelve in number, looking somewhat incongruous in that setting. Then it was explained to us; they were the Titanic survivors! And we moved along, shaking hands with them in turn. It was worth making the journey to London just for that.

In the auditorium, Kenneth More introduced the film from the stage.

In the space of the past two or three weeks I had developed a good appetite for the non-colour film which also starred Honor Blackman, Michael Goodliffe and David McCallum, with a running time of 118 minutes. It was a good film but with none of the main stars on-screen enough for a truly 'lead' role. I remember it more as a documentary-style film.

At the end of the performance our group was invited upstairs to join the VIPs. It was like a fairly large ballroom, not crowded, but 'busy', with space to circulate. In the centre was a small table on which was a reel-to-reel tape-recorder. Four chairs were provided - our seats while recordings for Radio Luxemburg of our interview were to be made.

Anthony Marriott held the mike, made the introduction and questioned me first; routine stuff - who I was, where I was from etc - and then asked, *"And what did you think of the film, Mr Hunter?"* I replied that I'd thought it wonderful. I went on,*"I was particularly impressed by Michael Goodliffe as the ship's designer. He was - "*

"Sorry, Geoff, sorry, but I've got to interrupt you there. We'll start the interview again but this time I think it would be wiser to praise Kenneth More. After all, he's the star of the film and we won't be treading on any

toes." So next time it was Kenneth More as the ship's second officer who I commended, to Mr Marriott's satisfaction.

As the young man from Chester was being interviewed, Tony nudged me and said, *"There's Kenneth More over there. Take this autograph book and pen and do what you can for my lads."*

Kenneth More, surprisingly, was standing alone and so isolated it appeared that a chalk circle had been drawn on the floor 12 feet in diameter with him standing in the centre seeming to defy all others to encroach on his domain. Undaunted, I approached him on his port side and spoke to his profile, noting that he was a few inches shorter than me.

"Congratulations, Mr More," I said, *"on a very fine film. I wonder if you'd be so kind as to sign this autograph book for my two young nephews?"* Still staring ahead he raised his left arm sideways, indicating that I was to put the book in his hand, which I did. Having signed the book, without a glance in my direction or a single word of comment he returned the autograph book to me with the same sideways movement he had received it, whereupon I acknowledged it with a polite, *"Thank you, Mr More."*

I returned to Tony, *"I managed to get it,"* I said, showing him the autograph, *"but I wasn't impressed with his manner."*

"I know, I was watching," he said. *"I'll tell you what it means, Geoff. When we get home you'll be able to say you met Kenneth More, but you won't be able to claim that Kenneth More met you!"*

I was disturbed by Kenneth More's compliant but contemptuous attitude but it was dispelled by my second and last approach with the autograph book that evening. Within minutes of returning to Tony I spotted popular singer Alma Cogan, together with three young gents in evening dress. Miss Cogan wore a stunning, shimmering, full length blue gown. I approached, then hesitated a moment, and as I did so she glanced, then turned fully to me and said rather sweetly, *"Can I help you?"* *"Indeed, you can, if you will, Miss Cogan. I'm hoping you'll sign my young nephews' autograph book."*

"But of course." She took the book, did what was necessary and then said, *'Would you mind telling me your name?"* *"It's Hunter,"* I answered. *"No, no, no,"* she feigned mild annoyance. *"I want to know your christian name."*

"I'm Geoff - with a 'G'."

"Well, Geoff, I must confess, you intrigue me. Where on earth have you brought that fascinating voice from? You're certainly not from around here."

An old British bus chugs up Hibel Road ...

... having just passed the entrance to Hibel Road station.

"I'm from Macclesfield, in Cheshire. 18 miles from Manchester."

"Now that leads to another question. Occasions like tonight's premiere are attended mainly by Londoners and showbiz folk. How did you manage to get invited?"

"I won a competition on Radio Luxemburg."

Alma's face lit up at this reply. *"Did you hear that fellas? Geoff's a competition winner. What did you have to do in this competition?"*

I explained that it was an interesting tale but would take too long to recount. *"We've plenty of time, haven't we fellas? You're not going to get away without telling us. Fire away."*

And so I spent the next 10 to 15 minutes detailing the whole story, at the end of which she said, gleefully, *"I bet those Radio Luxemburg people thought you had actually drawn the illustration."* I laughed at that. *"You're so right, but I've confessed to all my sins today."*

"Well, Geoff, that's a wonderful story. Now tell me what you thought of tonight's film."

I said, *"I thought it was very good indeed. I was particularly impressed by Michael Goodliffe as the ship's designer. He is perfect for that type of role."* (I did enjoy voicing my true sentiments!)

"Yes," she agreed, *"he was good, wasn't he! Now, how long are you staying in London, Geoff?"* she asked. I glanced at my watch. *"Only a few more minutes, I'm afraid. It's time Tony and I were making a dash for Euston Station."*

Alma was genuinely shocked to hear this. "What a dreadful shame that you've had to cram your visit all into one day! I was hoping that you'd be staying - if only for the week-end, at least."

I held out my hand in gratitude, and she clasped it, saying, *"Geoff, it's been such a pleasure to meet you... Have a safe journey home. Say 'goodbye' to Geoff, fellas."*

The warmth generated by Alma Cogan that evening, returns whenever I think of her; the memory of our only meeting cherished poignantly, for sadly, on 26th October, 1966, that very special lady succumbed to cancer. She was a mere thirty-four years of age. In her brief life she had enjoyed success. She was a regular guest on radio in Take it from Here, and had 20 song hits which included *Bell Bottom Blues, I Can't Tell a Waltz from a Tango, Dreamboat,* and *In the Middle of the House.*

14

Beaten by the Gun

Many Macclesfield folk will recall Mr Frank Yates, who conducted a chiropody business from his home - one of those fine upstanding stock-brick houses towards the top of Hobson Street.

I sought Mr Yates's help on only one occasion. Early one Monday evening, about 1962, I limped to his surgery expecting to be given an appointment to see him at a later date but he agreed to see me immediately.

Having explained the mystery of my painful foot I was instructed to divest my shoe and sock and he examined the sole of my foot with a magnifying glass.

"It's a verruca", he declared. *"You've probably picked it up at the public baths. Nothing to worry about. You've a choice here: I can remove it without any great discomfort to you over two or three visits or, if you are prepared to suffer a bit of pain this evening, I can remove it at one sitting. What's it to be?"*

With economy paramount in my mind I opted for punishment so, as I leaned back in my chair he sat opposite, my foot on his lap, cradled in his hands.

"What a beautifully shaped foot it is," he enthused. *"Could it be that you are into sport in some way?"*

I explained that up to a year or two previously I had been an active member of Macclesfield Harriers, but a footballing injury to an ankle had put paid to that pursuit.

"The signs of sporting life are clear", he said and then went on to tell me a curious tale that went something like this:

"My father was an outstanding athlete, a walker par excellence. I was named after him. Years ago race walking was a much bigger sport than it is today. With little traffic on the roads events were organised throughout the year and complemented with shorter distance racing on track and field sport days. In the years up to the first world war Dad dominated the Northern Counties' walking scene and would probably have competed in the 1916 Olympic Games but for the war. That was a big disappointment to him."

Tournament finals early 1960s.
Ken Farrar, Peter Jones, Brenda Bailey, Jack Perry, Geoffrey Hunter, Norman Hodson,
Brian Davenport, Margaret Lea, Christine Moss, Bill Tarbett, Eric and Donald Malkin, and Ron Benson.

"I remember also a story he told of a lesser disappointment but a more interesting tale for all that, when he had been entered for a two mile handicap event, one Wednesday evening at a stadium in Manchester. He was a factory worker and prior to finishing work at 6 o'clock that evening he donned his vest and shorts under his normal clothing to save time later, for time was of a premium. He raced to Hibel Road station with his sports bag, caught the first available train to Manchester and, once there, raced down the London Road slope and across the city to the stadium.

On entering the arena he was shocked to observe the walkers were all poised on their marks for his event. A split second later the starter's gun sounded and as the whole field got into its stride my father raced across the inside area of the track peeling off his clothing as he went and then, having reached the back mark, allotted to him because of his prowess, he toed it in a deliberate gesture and then set off in pursuit of the other competitors.

It was an eight lap race and slowly, one by one, he caught up with his adversaries and finally breasted the tape with a few yards to spare, elated with his success. His euphoria was short-lived. The starter ruled that Macclesfield competitor Frank Yates was disqualified! Why? Because, he said, my father's toe was not toeing his mark when the gun was fired. Evidently, the starter's word was law for Dad's protest was ignored."

This end to the story signalled the end of my session of treatment and, having been advised to keep the dressing dry for the next week, I was charged seven shillings and sixpence for my visit, a reasonable fee for those days.

There is a footnote (no pun intended) to this story. So interested had I been by this yarn that when I returned home I put pen to paper to write to the Sports Editor of the *Manchester Evening Chronicle* which featured a 'Readers Write' page every Saturday evening. This story, I felt, would be a likely candidate for selection later that week. I was proved right. On Saturday the Frank Yates story was published with a promise of fifteen shillings which arrived during the next week.

I could therefore claim to have had free verruca treatment and an extra seven and sixpence in my pocket -- not to mention a painless spring in my step!

15
A Liberal Tendency

Browsing through past copies of Old Macc the other day I came across the Charles Beresford photograph of the Liberal Club, Queen Victoria Street, and I was reminded of the many pleasurable hours I spent there during many years as a member.

From first joining the club in 1948 and throughout the 30 years I regularly attended, there were two key figures in control. Stan Hough was a secretary with remarkable organising ability. In his quiet and unassuming way he organised leagues for various sports, including football. He shopped shrewdly and tastefully for prizes and operated a Barnaby Savings Club from the Liberal Club office on Friday evenings throughout the year. His contribution to social life in Macclesfield for several decades is incredible.

The second of a pair of stalwarts was Horace Hatton, the club's steward. Sandy-haired and somewhat florid in complexion, Horace kept a very solid grip on his status as bar manager. Firm but fair, he would clamp down hard on any misbehaviour and allow a limited amount of licence to casual visitors. Any itinerant showing his face too often would be reminded that payment of annual subscriptions would improve the taste of the beer no end!

Over the years as a moderate table tennis and darts player and later as a purely social member I have much to be grateful for and many

The Liberal Club, Queen Victoria Street, part of the Brocklehurst Memorial hall. It was demolished in the second half of the 20th century to make way for a supermarket.

memories of those years. One such story is worth telling here.

One Wednesday evening - early in the I960s I think - 1 called in the club and joined two of my pals at the left side of the bar, close to where Horace had his bar-flap. These were the days before decimal coinage; when you could buy a pint of bitter for about 1s 4d and pay a similar price for ten Park Drive tipped. At the other end of the bar were three of the club's elder statesmen. Just six of us in total and Horace behind the bar as usual.

That the place was so quiet and that Stan Hough wasn't in his usual place at the bar nursing his half pint glass of bottled Guinness indicated that a club team or teams had an away match.

I emptied my glass, checked my loose change and moved across the room for a modest gamble on the one-armed bandit situated close to the piano which dear old Harold Yarwood, former conductor of the Opera House orchestra, coaxed into life each Saturday evening.

The bandit was one of the old-fashioned models with no electric input and no buttons to press at all. Its only claim to ostentation was a stainless steel tube for an arm and a black shiny ball for a hand. Its diet was sixpences only. Above the window showing the three reels of fruit motifs was listed the various combinations needed to win: permutations of cherries, oranges, lemons, melons, and three BAR emblems required to win the jackpot.

Beneath the reels window was the small window of the catchment container holding the jackpot, which seemed pretty full to me. I was prepared to risk two tanners only and having inserted the first I pulled the arm gently towards me, easing it through the point of resistance. The three reels spun, then stopped in turn, leaving me unimpressed at the display with not a BAR in sight. I fed the machine the second coin and pulled the arm gently towards the resistance point again, and then as I increased my pressure I swear I sensed something magical passing through my hand and arm. The reels spun... and the first reel stopped at BAR. Then came a second BAR.... and finally a third BAR!

Quickly, I did what I had seen others do before me. I pushed my tummy up against the small winnings cup; so small, in fact, that if you didn't seal it speedily tanners would be spewing out and dancing all over the floor.

I called to Horace for a tray and when it was brought to me I managed, with dexterity too difficult to describe, to catch the deluge of coins as I backed quickly away from the machine and carried my spoils triumphantly to the bar.

Horace lifted his bar-flap. *"Come through to my kitchen,"* he said.

"You'll be better counting it there." I invited my two pals to follow me and to do the counting and the three of us sat at Horace's scrubbed table with my pals building the sixpences into columns of ten while I sat back glowing warmly. Shortly afterwards Horace put his head round the door and I said: *"Can you fix us up with three pints of bitter, please? And get a drink for yourself. Oh, and give those others in there whatever they want."*

Horace frowned at that. *"Are you sure?"* he asked.

"Certainly," I replied, *"I don't want to leave anybody out."*

Normally, a jackpot would have been worth between £5 and £6. My total was slightly disappointing and having completed the count we sat back in our chairs enjoying our pint and carried on with our idle talk of earlier.

Eventually, Horace returned and queried the sum. His policy, I knew, was to hold on to the jackpot sixpences for change and pay out in notes and larger silver coins.

"£4 13s 6d, Horace," I responded. *"Not so much as I'd hoped for."*

"You owe me 2s 8d," he said.

"Come, come, Horace," I smiled, *"Your arithmetic is letting you down. We've each had a pint of bitter, you've had a drink as well, and those in the bar have joined us."*

"I'm not wrong," said Horace. *"It's you that's wrong. The 2s 8d you owe me is in addition to the money on the table."*

"Aye, and you can pull the other one as well," I smiled. It was not often that Horace displayed such a sense of humour.

He gripped me gently by the upper arm, inviting me to rise from my chair. I did so and he beckoned me to follow him through the door to the bar area. That came as a shock to me. The place was full. There seemed to be fifty or sixty people there, all quietly sipping at their drinks.

"They've all had a drink on you," he said. *"I did ask you if it was all right and you gave me the okay."*

"True enough, Horace," I conceded, *"but where on earth have they all come from?"*

"They're from the Brocklehurst Memorial Hall. They usually pop in here when the Bingo finishes.

And don't forget....."

"I know, Horace, I know," I said resignedly, as I reached into my pocket, *"I owe you 2s 8d."*

16
Majestic Offerings

FOLKS who have read most of my reflections on the early days of my life, will know of the great love I had for the cinema as a boy. Just before the war I spent time each week cutting out of the News of the World the weekly film reviews. That was if I could get possession of the paper between all the family having read it and it being used as tinder for the fire. You could say I was Hollywood mad; a magical place I longed to visit, and every cigarette card bearing a film star's image was a treasured possession.

When Gran came to live with us, round about 1938, and 1 was selected to accompany her to the Cinema on Buxton Road each Thursday evening, that was a real bonus for me. As a lad of eleven, up to that point I had attended evening performances on only a few occasions; to achieve this joy on a regular weekly basis was to transform my world into Utopia! The thrill of cinema-going stayed with me for a good many years but at some point, gradually, the appeal began to pall.

Technologically, there had been great advances in film-making - today's special effects, for example, are astonishing and at times breathtaking - but it was the subject matter that began to cause me offence. There was (and still is) too much violence and death depicted and, currently, this fault is aggravated by slow-motion destruction and the crudest language - and I write as a man who had three years of barrack-room life during and after the war.   In the good old days when Macclesfield had five cinemas and Bollington had one of its own, it was the Majestic which reigned supreme. Built in 1922 it was the grandest one of all. If the Cinema, Premier and Regal clientele was mainly parochial, the Majestic, and to a lesser degree the Picturedrome, were more 'cosmopolitan'.

The Majestic had an opulence denied all the others and although this was a strong virtue in itself, the main attraction was that it brought to the town the top films of the day soon after they were released.

That our Country's cinemas were a great morale booster during the war and a most effective weapon of propaganda, there can be no doubt. Following the declaration of war on 3rd September, 1939, and the temporary

closing of all theatres, the Government relented speedily and Macclesfield's cinemas re-opened on Saturday, 9 September. but with a 10pm closing ruling. Just two weeks earlier, incidentally, thousands of women and children evacuees had arrived in Macclesfield in the first phase of this massive operation.

New Year's Day, 1940, was a wartime beginning to the year, following 21 years of peace. Looking back briefly, we can appreciate just what a momentous year in our history it was: Mr Churchill replaced Mr Chamberlain as Prime Minister; the BEF at Dunkirk carried out the greatest rear-guard action ever fought in history during the closing days of May and the first week of June; the occupation of France was completed by Germany two weeks later, and the Battle of Britain reached its height on 15th August with 180 German planes shot down. Throughout it all, the severely rationed British public tightened its belt, dangled its gas mask from hand or shoulder, picked its way carefully through the blackout, and went to the pictures....

As a Central Schoolboy at the time I recall a Ministry of Information van drawing up at the school, probably by prior arrangement. When the back of the van was opened it displayed a large cinema screen. With back-projection, films were shown and could be seen easily in daylight as we crowded behind the van like a Punch and Judy audience.

For many families, sweethearts and friends, visits to the cinema in those times were brief, sweet interludes, as those serving our country returned home on a weekend pass or a short period of embarkation leave. Dunkirk veterans returned home for a mere seven days before re-joining their units for another crack at Jerry. A wonderful buoyant spirit prevailed at all times and happy memories were stored despite the war and, sometimes because of it.

I am hopeful that a study of the rich menu of the Majestic film-fare for 1940 will bring back to some readers specific blissful memories, and serve also as a reminder of what a veritable oasis each cinema and theatre was in those troubled times.

Commencing Monday

JANUARY 1: *THE LION HAS WINGS* Ralph Richardson, Merle Oberon.
JAN 8: *WUTHERING HEIGHTS* Laurence Olivier, Merle Oberon.
JAN 15: *THE SUN NEVER SETS* Douglas Fairbanks Jnr, Barbara O'Neill.

The Majestic, one year after it was open, is the white building
on the left going up Mill Street.

JAN 22: *JAMAICA INN* Charles Laughton, Maureen O'Hara.
JAN 29: *NURSE EDITH CAVELL* Anna Neagle, George Sanders.

FEBRUARY 5: *STANLEY AND LIVINGSTONE* Spencer Tracey, Nancy Kelly
FEB 12: *ONLY ANGELS HAVE WINGS* Cary Grant, Jean Arthur.
FEB 19: *CAPTAIN FURY* Brian Aherne, June Lang.
FEB 26: *LAUGH IT OFF* Tommy Trinder, Jean Colin.

MARCH 4: *TIlE MAN IN THE IRON MASK* Louis Hayward, Joan Bennett.
MARCH 11: *THE FROZEN LIMITS* The Crazy Gang.
MARCH 18: *SUSANNAH OF THE MOUNTIES* Shirley Temple, Randolph Scott
MARCH 25: *COME ON GEORGE!* George Formby, Pat Kirkwood.

APRIL 1: *THE RAINS CAME* Myrna Loy, Tyrone Power.
APRIL 8: *FIRST LOVE* Deanna Durbin. Robert Stack.
APRIL 15: *THE OLD MAID* Bette Davies, George Brent
APRIL 22: *RULERS OF THE SEA* Douglas Fairbanks Jnr, Margaret Lockwood

MAY 6: *FOR FREEDOM* Will Fyffe, Anthony Hulme.
MAY 13: *GULLIVERS TRAVELS* Max Fleisher Cartoon.
MAY 20: *BABES IN ARMS* Mickey Rooney, Judy Garland.
MAY 27: *BAND WAGON* Arthur Askey.

JUNE 3: *NINOTCHKA* Greta Garbo. Melvyn Douglas.
JUNE 10: *THE PROUD VALLEY* Paul Robeson, Rachel Thomas.
JUNE 17: *BALALAIKA* Nelson Eddy, Ilona Massey.
JUNE 24: *DESTRY RIDES AGAIN* James Stewart, Marlene Dictrich.

JULY 1: *THE WIZARD OF OZ* Judy Garland, Frank Morgan.
JULY 8: *MR SMITH GOES TO WASHINGTON* James Stewart, Jean Arthur.
JULY 15: *THE EARL OF CHICAGO* Robert Montgomery, Edward Arnold.
JULY 22: *ANOTHER THIN MAN* William Powell, Myrna Loy.
JULY 29: *THE INVISIBLE MAN RETURNS* Vincent Price, Nan Grey.

AUGUST 5: *CONTRABAND* Conrad Veidt, Valerie Hobson.
AUGUST 12: *HIS GIRL FRIDAY* Cary Grant, Rosalind Russell.
AUGUST 19: *TIlE BLUE BIRD* Shirley Temple, Nigel Bruce.
AUGUST 26: *CHARLEY'S BIGHEARTED AUNT* Arthur Askey, Phyllis Calvert

SEPTEMBER 2: *MERRY GO ROUND* On the stage Variety Show.
SEPT 9: *LET GEORGE DO IT* George Formby, Phyllis Calvert.

SEPT 16: *STRANGE CARGO* Joan Crawford, Clark Gable.
SEPT 23: *IT'S A DATE* Deanna Durbin, Walter Pidgeon.
SEPT 30: *SWANEE RIVER* Don Ameche, Andrea Leeds.

OCT 7: NORTH-WEST PASSAGE Spencer Tracy, Ruth Hussey.
OCT 14: *THE GRAPES OF WRATH* Henry Fonda, Jane Darwell.
OCT 21: *ROAD TO SINGAPORE* Crosby, Hope, Lamour.
OCT 28: *TYPHOON* Dorothy Lamour, Robert Preston.

NOVEMBER 4: *PINOCCHIO* Walt Disney Classic.
NOV 11: *HUNCHBACK OF NOTRE DAME* Charles Laughton, Maureen O'Hara
NOV 18: *EDISON THE MAN* Spencer Tracy, Rita Johnson.
NOV 25: *PASTOR HALL* Wilfred Lawson, Nova Pilbeam.

DECEMBER 2: *CONVOY* Clive Brook, John Clements.
DEC 9: *THE FRIGHTENED LADY* Marius Goring, Helen Haye.
DEC 16: *FORTY LITTLE MOTHERS* Eddie Cantor, Judith Anderson.
DEC 23: *SOMEWHERE IN ENGLAND* Frank Randle, Harry Korris.
DEC 30: *NEW MOON* Nelson Eddy, Jeanette MacDonald.

17
Stranger in the Night

I would be the first to admit that the story I have to tell, a true tale of only 32 years ago, hardly places it in the Old Macc category in terms of vintage. But I have kept it to myself for far too long and wish now to share it with our readers.

It was, I believe, the first Monday of February, 1973, and I was sitting quietly by the fire following tea, having completed another day's work in the design department, Barrack Fabrics, in my 25th year of service to the company. My daughter, Lorraine, within weeks of her sixteenth birthday, was out with her friends.

I discerned the faint ring of my front door bell. I switched on the hall light and opened the door. A man, a stranger, was standing there, and as he started to speak I silenced him with a quick insistence to come inside, out from the cold. I invited him to sit on the settee while I returned to my armchair.

He started to speak again and I felt bound to interrupt him. *"Before you say anything,"* I interjected, *"let me put you in the picture regarding myself at the moment. I am suffering from an infection in both my ears. In the normal way of things I am rather deaf and wear a hearing aid, but as I cannot wear the aid whilst I am receiving treatment, the situation is particularly difficult for me. What I propose is that I share the settee with you and must ask that you speak loudly in order to state your business. Okay?"*

The reader will understand the normal embroidery to conversation had to be dispensed with and since I made numerous interruptions, for the sake of clarity, I intend now to refine the telling of the story for the readers convenience.

The man was, I should think, probably between 35 and 40 and of smart appearance. He had arrived by car, as I had already noted, and he was in an anxious state. His name, he said, was David Shepherd - I am guessing at the spelling - and I remarked how famous a name it was since we already had a batsman bishop and a wild-life artist with the same name.

He had recently been made redundant, he said, and I got the impression he had been deeply hurt by the severance and, since he had the appearance of a company director, he had probably lost a very good job.

He was philosophical. Life had to go on and he was now seeking another avenue of employment. To this end he produced from his person (or from his case) a transparent bag, six inches by four, containing a stiff coloured display card which completely filled the bag, and a plastic object which he slid out of the bag into the palm of his hand.

"This,' he said, holding it out to me, *"is a tube holder and dispenser. Anything that is sold in a tube, be it toothpaste, ointment, glue, artists' colour or whatever, if used in conjunction with this clever idea will ensure there is no wastage. The bottom end of the tube fits into this slot and while the tube is in use you just keep turning the key here so that, progressively, the flattened tube is wound round and round the drum in the base and nothing is wasted. This is a German product and you'll note the coloured card inside the bag is printed in German. It is this card that has brought me here tonight.*

"On Thursday morning this week I have to go by train to London and I have to take with me an English copy of this card -- I have the English

translation of the card here. At the meeting I am due to attend I hope to be granted the franchise to sell the tube holder in this country. Unfortunately, so far, I have been unable to find an artist to produce the card in English and I'm getting really desperate now.

"Someone this afternoon suggested that Dale's art shop on Park Green might advise me and the man there said the only person he could think of was you and he gave me your address. You are my last hope - honest."

I pointed out to David that it was rather late in the day for such an undertaking, given that I was working full time as it was. *"You are asking me to do it in two evenings - tomorrow and Wednesday."*

"But you could do it, couldn't you, in the two nights?" he insisted. *"Please, please say you could. You are my last chance. I know I have no right imposing on you in this way but it is so important to my future."*

"There is another point I've got to make," I said. *"All this small lettering on the card, both black and white. At this late point I would have to use Copenhagen Script. It is an alternative style but its main virtue is that I can produce it fairly speedily."*

"You'll do it for me then, won't you?" he pleaded.

I acquiesced. *"I'll give it a try. I should be able to plan it out tomorrow evening and be ready to paint in the detail on Wednesday."*

He was profuse in his thanks. *"What time do you want me to come Wednesday evening to collect it?"*

"Make it ten o' clock," I replied, *"but be prepared to wait if necessary. It's all very iffy at the moment."*

The man took his leave, greatly relieved, and I sat studying the German card and mentally planned my strategy for two evenings of labour. When my daughter Lorraine came in later we discussed this unexpected commission. *"There's this about it, Dad. Tomorrow I've arranged to go to the pictures and on Wednesday evening I've a meeting at Bethel Baptist. so I won't be under your feet."*

The next morning a rare event occurred: the post arrived before I'd left for work. Just one letter concerning a serious family problem and what bit of wind I had had in my sails quickly dissipated, but I had a duty to my employer and to fulfil my pledge of the previous night. I sacrificed my lunch hour that day to stroll into town and buy white ink for David's commission.

That evening, my planning phase, though time-consuming, went well and by 10.30 1 was all set up for the morrow. Following Wednesday's work at Barracks I settled for a quick bowl of soup with bread for tea and was mixing colour by 6.30, and on my way...

Because of the cold temperature I had chosen to work in my sitting room with the table close to the fire. I am not the tidiest of workers when under pressure and as the evening progressed the floor became more and more strewn with bits of sample colourings and tracing debris. At precisely 9.55, just as I considered the job completed, the faint ringing of my door-bell seemed to signify a perfect night's planning with the customer dead on time.

I was wrong. The caller was my St John Ambulance colleague, Bill Tarbett. I asked him in and he surveyed my untidy floor with dismay. *"Not to worry Bill,"* I said, *"I'll explain this as I tidy up."*

Bill, it seems, had been at a loose end and hoped I could find time to share a drink with him at our usual watering-hole, The Lord Byron. I put the room to rights and placed the old and new display cards in an envelope on the mantelpiece, when Lorraine arrived back from her Baptist meeting.

"Lorraine will attend to things for me," I said to Bill. *"Look, Lorraine, Mr Shepherd is due to call any minute. You'll have to ask him in - you can trust him - and his completed job is in that envelope. Tell him the fee is £4 and if he wishes to see me I shall be at the Lord Byron."*

I felt I had earned a pint and we found the Byron virtually empty. Bill and I sat just inside a room on the left with Bill nearest the bar, just feet away, able to hear if my name was mentioned. Trade remained quiet and at 11-15 we took our leave. Bill dropped me off at home and I entered the house. Lorraine was still up watching the telly. The envelope was no longer on the mantelpiece.

"Mr Shepherd's been then?" I asked. *"Yes."* replied Lorraine, *"but haven't you seen him?"* I shook my head. *"That's strange, very strange,"* she said and told her story.

Mr Shepherd had come just minutes after I had left with Bill, and asked about his art-work. She had handed him the envelope and he had studied both sides of the new card. *"Marvellous!"* he had exclaimed, at which point Lorraine informed him the fee was £4 and if he wished to see me he could do so. *"Dad's at the Lord Byron with a pal. That's straight down Windmill*

Street to the bottom and carry on up Chapel Street on the other side and the Byron is just on the left."

"Yes, yes, I know where the Lord Byron is," he said. "I'll go straight away and pay your father myself and thank him for his help. And thank you very much. Goodnight."

Lorraine broke the uneasy silence. "Maybe with it being rather late, Dad, he decided to call on you another night at a more reasonable time." I consoled myself that was the most likely explanation.

But it didn't happen. I have never seen David Shepherd since and I never did get my £4 fee, which would be worth ten times that amount today. And yet, I have never been able to accept the mysterious Mr Shepherd - however he spells his name - deliberately let me down. Call me naive if you will, but I remember the man's deep anxiety, his earnest pleading and his immense relief and expressions of gratitude when I agreed to help him.

What did happen, I wonder, after he left my home at 10.15 that Wednesday evening, his problems behind him?

Perhaps now that I have told my story, that question will be answered.

18
Auld Acquaintance

I warmed to this pantomime programme when my dear old pal, Ken Miller, brought it and other items of his family's theatrical life for me to study.

Chris Paling, Jean Patterson, Ken's sister Joan and his mother Anne, are remembered by locals with a fondness for the theatre, for they impressed themselves indelibly on Macclesfield's entertainment scene for a good many years with their true professional ability.

John Worsley, always a close friend, was at this time in his life quite new to the theatre. He had developed into a superb table tennis player - a talent, he once told me, he would have been happy to exchange just to be able to play a competent game of football. As a semi-professional entertainer John went on to become a mime artist second to none. His early death was a grievous loss to our world.

Frankie Woods and Tiny Little, who were actually Frank Hargreaves and Alan Wood, came together as a double act in the 1930s. Frank borrowed

Alan's surname and added an 's' and Alan's choice of stage name matched his zany style of humour. They were both employed by Barracks Fabrics, Frank dealing with the chemical side of the business and Alan as a printer. Of the two Frank was clearly the more versatile and eventually became a full-time professional children's entertainer, with his wife Barbara. When appearing locally he also had strong support from pianist Alice Axford and Harold Swindells. Together with his wife, Harold also gave such stout service to St John Ambulance Brigade.

Barbara Hosker (Red Riding Hood) is another name to bring back memories. This charmer lived at 149 Black Road. In or about 1953, Barbara and her mum (a staunch Liberal) were in the audience at the Brocklehurst Memorial Hall when I took the stage as Mark Anthony. The Macclesfield Liberal Party had organised a conference at which the guest of honour was Sir Philip Fothergill, Chairman of the Party. As entertainment, Mr Walter Simon, a prominent member, planned a Young Liberals' presentation of Act 3, Scene 2 of Shakespeare's *Julius Caesar* - the famous funeral scene - and had invited members of the Liberal club table tennis section to provide maturity to the cast. Bernard Kinsella, Jim Worth, myself and others were happy to oblige. We joined forces with Paul Rathbone, son of Clifford, editor of the Macclesfield Express, who had already made several broadcasts in plays on BBC radio, Charles and Hannah Simon and Clare Doncaster, daughter of the prospective Liberal candidate for Macclesfield, and all their friends.

I recall joining Barbara Hosker and her mum after the performance with a great sense or relief for I had narrowly escaped two disasters on stage. Shortly before taking my place on the dais for Caesar's funeral oration I was handed the scroll of Caesar's will. The scroll was fastened with red ribbon which had been stapled to it and tied in a bow. With hindsight, I should have untied the ribbon and retied it to my satisfaction. I simply tucked it into the folds of my toga.... then, with moments to go, someone spotted I was still wearing my wrist watch. Hardly in 44 BC!

On stage, and ten minutes into my funeral speech, I informed the Friends, Romans and Countrymen, as I produced the scroll, *"Here is the will, and under Caesar's seal."* I tugged at a loose end of the ribbon's bow and it refused to budge. It had obviously been tied a second time.There was no time for fiddling; I hooked a finger inside the looped ribbon and give it a

Centenary School, Macclesfield

The Patterson Stage School

presents the Pantomime

"Red Riding Hood"

Saturday, 21st February, 1948

at 7-0 p.m.

Producer ...	...	...	...	...	Chris Paling
Stage Manager	...	...	...	...	K. Kreves
Lighting	...	...	...	...	J. Gilmore
Costumes	...	...	...	Smith & Co. Ltd.
Scenery ...	...	...	...	Stage Furnishing Ltd.
Make-up	...	...	...	...	B. Patterson

Orchestra under the direction of Mrs. A. Miller.

Chairman : Mr. Fred Collier.

in aid of Brunswick Trust Funds

CAST

Robin Hood	...	...	...	Jean Patterson
Maid Marion	...	...	...	Joan Savage
Dame Trot	...	...	...	...Joan Miller
Red Riding Hood	...	...	...	Barbara Hosker
Simple Simon	...	...	...	John Worsley
Baron Hardup	...	...	...	Jack Hoyle
Tom } Broker's Men ...		...	...	Franky Woods
Tim }				Tiny Little
The Wolf	...	...	...	Redvers Savage
Jack Horner	...	...	...	Ann Rende
Miss Muffett	...	...	...	Joyce Hatton
Corlina	...	...	...	Gwen Clayton
The Witch	...	...	...	Gordon Avery
Tishy	...	...	...	{ Harold Patterson } Ron Hatton

Gnomes, Villagers, Retainers, etc.

General Ensemble, Ballet and Specialities by
Miss Jean Patterson, M.R.A.D, U.K.A.P.T.D. (Hons),
N.A.T.D. (Tap Hons).

short, firm snatch, and said a quick prayer. The ribbon came away leaving the scroll intact and I was able to inform the Citizens of Rome, with considerable relief, just what a great benefactor Caesar had been to them.

Other local artistes' names which spring to mind from those early Chris Paling productions are Leslie Biggar, Phil Corke. Rhona Walton, Hilary Martin, Grant Turner, Jim Chatterton, Bill Davison, Norman Clarke, Geoff Morris, Graham Carroll, Joan Southern. Janice Hosker and Ken Whittaker. Not forgetting the acrobatic team: Norman Bingham, Jack Burgess and Lynda Moss.

In closing I wish to take this opportunity to pay tribute to Anne Miller. who is no longer with us. A pianist all her life, she passed her first exam at the age of six. At the time of the 1914-18 war she entertained the troops and accompanied the silent films of that era and many celebrities when radio came into being. Through the years many pupils passed through her hands.

Anne came to Macclesfield in 1930 and for many years was musical director for the local repertory theatre. She then went on to play for the wartime choir, conducted by Wilf Hammond and accompanied many guest celebrities including Olive Groves, George Baker and Huw Weldon. Joined by her violinist husband she entertained Queen Wilhelmina of the Netherlands at Capesthorne Hall.

Anne started the Macclesfield Amateur Variety Artists who put on pantomimes and charity shows, and was musical director for the original Majestic Players and Holmes Chapel and Wilmslow Operatic Society. She was organist for the Spiritualist Church for 40 years and played for the Central School for Girls for 35 years.

In all, Anne devoted a full 50 years to Macclesfield and deserves to be remembered with affection and gratitude.

19
Misplaced Credit

A few years ago I helped organise a Macclesfield Harriers' 1950s and 1960s reunion evening held at The Travellers' Rest, Cross Street. A great night - the old pals came from far and wide. We grouped and re-grouped throughout the evening, reliving the glorious past.

At some point, late in the evening - Jack, I think it was -said to me. *"Remember that time at Uttoxeter Sports, the year Sidney Wooderson presented the prizes and you won the half-mile?"*

I shook my head. *"You're wrong, Jack - I came fifth that day."*

"No, no. It's you that's wrong", he insisted. He called Fred over. *"Fred, I bet you remember Geoff winning the half-mile at Uttoxeter, don't you?"*

"I do that!" said Fred, addressing me. *"And you were spiked in the heel in the semis and had to have treatment before you could contest the final."*

"You are right about the spiking," I confirmed, *"but the truth is I finished fifth - and it was nothing to do with the injury - I ran a good race, actually."*

"Geoff," said Jack, *"your memory's playing tricks with you. You had a run of successes at that time. You beat Stockport's Fitzsimmons in the Bosley mile, and you....."*

"Wrong again!" I felt bound to protest. *"Fitzsimmons was on the 195 mark that day and I failed by about six yards to catch him."*

"I recall those days so well," Jack mused, ignoring my denial, *"and what a time we had at the inaugural Disley Fell race, running from the village then up to Lyme Cage......"*

"Ah," I smiled, *"now you're really on my wavelength."* Flashes of that wonderful day came to mind. That Saturday evening when I returned home and put the shiny barometer into my mother's hands. *"How's that for the hall wall, Mum?"* I had said and she had looked at it in awe. *"Is it first prize you've won, our Geoff?"* she had asked. *"That it is, Mum"*, I replied proudly.

"By heck, our Geoff," she had said. *"You'll have your name in t' News o' World tomorrow!"* And she was right...

Jack was continuing with his story. *"Some climb that was, up to the Cage and round it, and then we had that fast downwards run and back up to the lane and to the finish. You finished sixth, Geoff, and I was eighth."*

"Jack," I said wearily, *"don't you think it's time you went for your bus?"*

20
All the Fun of the 'Fare'

It was during the early to late Thirties that Macclesfield's twice-yearly fair had the most appeal for me.

On the Friday evening of fair week my normal ha'penny 'spends' would be doubled to a full penny and I could contemplate with relish the value I hoped to receive for it.

The reader must not underestimate the importance of that single copper coin. At that time it represented, for example, 2 ounces of sweets - and it could have been used for that purpose - but sweets aren't 'fair', are they? Ice cream could be classed as 'fair' for Granelli's had a regular spot close to the café on the Millstone corner and I could have had one small cornet early in the evening and another some time later. But I don't recall ever doing so. There were alternatives you see.... To a background of steam organ music one could buy peanuts in their shells at a penny a bag, or enjoy a thrilling roundabout ride for the same price, or a swing on either the big boats or the rope-propelled shallow craft usually located close to the sheep pens by Buxton Road bridge, with its Cookson's Garage advertisement.

Gambling was catered for with the perennial circular roll-a-penny stalls where the stallholder had a square mirror handy as proof that your penny **was** clipping a black line. You could play the odds by putting your money on a coloured area on an oil-cloth covered table and hope the dart thrower hit one of your segments on a rapidly spinning wooden disc. Balls could be rolled down sloping tables into numbered slots, but only certain totals could win and prizes were paltry. In the later years a celluloid ball landing in a goldfish bowl would win a goldfish and hooking a numbered duck with rod and line won you a chalky ornament.

I remember one little old fair lady, shawl draped over her head, who told customers their fortunes in a novel way. She carried in front of her a narrow wooden tray suspended from her neck by a stout cord. The tray incorporated a slotted money box, a thin dowel rod from one side to the other, and beneath it space for several hundred slips of paper bearing news of glad tidings and lucky numbers and colours. Her untethered pet canary

Life above the Dams steps.

Geoffrey and family pose for a press photograph following a trade contest win in 1959.

Below the Dams steps - flooding in Elizabeth Street. Geoffrey's near neighbours were so prone to occasional flooding the doorways had permanent stone sills as a defence.

perched on the dowel and whenever a client dropped a penny into the box the bird would bow sharply, pluck a slip of paper from below with its beak and proffer it to the customer.

One year I had a hankering to win a coconut prize. I could visualise what a proud moment it would be, going home to Waterloo Street and saying: *"Look what I won in the fair!"* There were few openings where one could win a nut for a mere penny but one such was a stall opposite Edmund Lomas's mill where the hard rough surface of the ground swept gently downwards from Central Station to the kerb (there was no shallow wall there in those days).

It was first and foremost a tin cans and duster-missiles stall, but had as a side-line a ball-in-a-pail challenge. The pail was slotted between two rungs of a short piece of ladder and angled at floor level with its open mouth facing the customer some six feet away behind the toe-board. A penny bought a wooden ball, normally used at the coconut shy, and to win, the ball had to be thrown into the pail and stay there. It seemed easy but it had already been pointed out to me many times how difficult it was. What was recommended was a fairly firm throw, hitting the pail high on the side to enable the ball to spiral downwards to exhaust its energy.

Not surprisingly, my effort was a classic 'how not to do it' for the ball hit the base of the pail with such a resounding plonk and bounced out with such alacrity I instantly went into a state of shock. Early in the evening, though it was, I returned home a totally demoralised, but wiser lad.

On another occasion my penny got me into the boxing tent, a concession that surprised me. No local aspirant had come forward at that session to dispute prowess and the fair pugilists had to fight each other. Two lethargic elders of this ilk spent most of three rounds facing each other on one side of the ring, gripping the top rope for support with one gloved hand and clubbing each other unscientifically with the other. Not a pretty sight... Following this charade the promoter came round with his inverted trilby begging the spectators to show appreciation for *"two game lads"*. You had to smile.

Another time my penny booked me a ringside position at a Flea Circus the only time I ever knew it to visit our fair, which explains its allure for me. The sporting arena for these creatures was a card table and once the ringmaster (for want of a better term) was in position, with a dozen of us crowding round, the little booth was packed. There was no delay - the man was 'itching' to get started - and soon there were fleas pulling tiny chariots, walking the tight-rope and doing all manner of clever stunts. I remember ensuring I breathed in a gentle way as I leaned forward totally captivated, conscious that a sharp intake of breath might suck one of the little blighters into my mouth or nose.

The show I failed to see was when the beheaded lady came to town. It was a May fair and a group of us lads clustered close to the stage from where a straight-faced barker delivered a remarkable story of a medical phenomenon; a tale, let it be said, that owed much to coincidence. The beautiful girl, lying inside the tent behind him, he claimed, had recently been walking sedately along a Paris street when she was suddenly decapitated cleanly in a freak accident. How the accident occurred was not explained but luckily for the girl an eminent surgeon had witnessed the tragedy and with black bag in hand rushed to the still body and was surprised to find the heart still beating. Luckier still, he chanced to be carrying in his bag several lengths of rubber tubing, and although unhopeful of success, connected the arteries and veins of the main body to those of the head. Amazingly, life in the head returned and now, on show for the first time in the British Isles, for the price of a single penny, Macclesfield folk could witness the paralysed body of this young woman connected by tubes to the living head!

I and one or two of my pals were out of funds by this time (perhaps it was the time the fleas had won my vote) but a couple of the lads went in to satisfy their curiosity, the rest of us waiting outside for their report. Presently - and surprisingly - there was the sound of laughter issuing from within and shortly afterwards our pals emerged to denounce the whole thing as a fiddle. This came as no surprise to me. Predictably, there were two wholesome young ladies involved in the deception - one clad theatrically in a brief sparkling costume, her legs exposed, lay on her back on a divan with her head strained right back over the top edge. A rubber pad was fastened to the front of her neck from which four rubber tubes led to the rubber collar of another girl sitting in a Turkish bath type of box with just her head protruding above. The rubber collar served the dual purpose of housing the four tubes and sealing the gap around her neck. Folds of artificial silk or satin covered the prostrate girl's head to complete the illusion.

But what about the laughter? I wanted to know. Well, it seemed the 'headless' one of this gruesome twosome had brought with her to

Macclesfield a skin irritation and was unable to lie perfectly still as
instructed. Her vigorous scratching of both thighs had seemed to her amused
audience totally out of keeping with the macabre tableau. What's more,
tickled by her friend's discomfort. the head on the box, vibrating with
suppressed mirth. added to the general merriment. Now, if she had had an
itchy nose...

21
Louisa's Clogs

In October 1994 I had the good fortune to make the acquaintance of a lady
with a very interesting past. I was introduced to Mrs Louisa Higginbotham,
a widow, by my very good friend, floral artist Edith Buxton, at her home
Blakelow Cottage. Also present were Mrs Edith Henshaw whose late
husband, Phillip, had shared a great deal of my working life and Mrs Nancy
Brocklehurst, nee Hadfield who started school with me at Trinity Square on
the very same day in 1931.

By arrangement, Louisa (I use her christian name out of fondness,
rather than familiarity) a childhood friend of Mrs Buxton, had brought with
her numerous photographs from times past for us to peruse. From her bag
she also produced a miniature pair of clogs, bewitching in their charm. The
leather had stiffened with time but each was perfectly intact with irons, split
tongue and clasp fasten. But more about their history later.

Under the venerable beams in the snug little olde worlde parlour, as the
coffee flowed, so did the anecdotes as we nibbled savoury biscuits, buttered
scones and chocolate cake. Delightful! Louisa proved to be a most
charming, colourful character with a wealth of stories to tell of her life.

Her family roots went back to Ireland and I calculate that about 1870
the O'Connor family, which included a lad of 10 who would later become
Louisa's father, made the move to England to improve its lot. At some stage
during the journey the first O in their name was dropped and they became
the Connor family, perhaps in the belief that with a more indigenous profile
more doors of opportunity would he opened to them.

They came first to Prestbury but as the years passed and the lad grew
up he married and became domiciled at Oldham He joined what was, or

came to be, the Showman's Guild and through the years toured with the fairs with his coconut shy and hoop-la stalls, taking his wife and constantly increasing family with him in a caravan. By the time Louisa was born in November 1906 she was the eighth child. In 1909 when the family arrived in Macclesfield with the May fair the mother was heavily pregnant again.

At this point, to ease the pressure of family circumstances, Louisa's father entered into an agreement, whereby his youngest child would stay, temporarily, with Mr and Mrs Swindells of 43 Waterloo Street, and be collected later on the journey back to Oldham. No money changed hands. It was a christian gesture not uncommon in those days.

Louisa in 1996 at Trinity Home

The sequel to this part of the story is tragic. During the continuance of the fair's tour the lives of the mother and the child she was expecting were lost during the confinement and on the father's return to Macclesfield the Swindells family's offer to continue looking after young Louisa until such time as he called to collect her, was accepted.

In the event, the other seven children were, in their turn, fostered out to other families and Louisa was to remain in the bosom of the Swindells family until her marriage.

Louisa's father remained in close contact with her. She recalls that each time the fair came to Macclesfield her dad would collect her, allow her to savour the full joy of the entertainment, and return her to her Waterloo Street home with her arms laden with goodies.

Fence Sunday School provided the early religious instruction for Louisa, being a matter of mere yards from her home, and early in 1911 she began her formal education at Daybrook Street School. In those days it was a mixed primary school accommodating pupils for three years only. From there she moved to Beech Lane and finally, to complete her education, she attended Athey Street School, with which at the age 12 she alternated as a part-time worker at Hurdsfield Mills.

One particular story of her Athey Street days came readily to Louisa's mind. One Monday morning she was on her way to school with her friend, Florrie Hulse, when, having arrived at the bottom of the 108 steps, Waters Green, they spent a short time probing the enclosed area on the left - the Nags Head pub was on the other side - where the rotten fruit and vegetables from the Saturday market were customarily deposited before removal. Louisa unearthed a fair-sized orange which, although soft, still remained spherical with its peel intact.

Very much a tom-boy, she instructed her friend Florrie to stand at the angle of the turn, part way up the steps, while she climbed further up the steps to a spot where the bottom was not visible to her. She would hurl the orange downs the steps and it would be Florrie's task to observe from her vantage point how far the fruit was thrown.

Well, Louisa did her stuff, aiming for the blind area where she considered the bottom of the steps to be. She observed the orange's descent until it vanished from view then focussed her eyes on Florrie for the verdict.

Suddenly, Florrie started, and came running hastily up the steps. *"Quick,"* she gasped to Louisa, *"Run. You've hit a woman."* So they ran, soon making up the time they had lost. Once at school they had just recovered their breath in the classroom when their teacher received a message that the headmaster, Mr Gaskell (Daddy Gaskell to the pupils) wished to see Louisa Connor in his study.

"I say", she whispered to Florrie as she got to her feet to comply, *"perhaps he's going to make me a prefect"*, but when she had tapped on the head's study door and been bidden to enter, visions of a prefect's status dissipated. She found to her consternation that Mr Gaskell was not alone. Seated close to his desk was a young lady, refinely-dressed, and wearing a broad-brimmed white hat, with an orange splodge on its crown!

Louisa recognised her as Miss Birchenough, daughter of the Victoria Park keeper of Park Lodge, Buxton Road. It would seem this unforgiving and resourceful maiden had chased after and followed the two girls and

A coffee morning at Edith Buxton's Blakelow Cottage July 11th 1994, Edith's 86th birthday. From L to R: Edith, Marion Swindells, John Swindells, Peggy (Margaret) Leigh and Geoffrey. It was at such a morning that Geoffrey met Louisa Higginbotham.

supplied the headmaster with sufficient information to identify the culprit.

A profound apology was tendered and Louisa was given the onerous task of reminding herself, one hundred times in writing, that respectable young ladies do not misbehave!

After leaving school Louisa continued working for BWA on a full-time basis. During her teens her father gave up his nomadic life and chose a more stable occupation. Louisa was able to visit him for holidays and enjoy periods of family togetherness.

At her coming-of-age her father presented her with the miniature clogs previously referred to. They were, he said, the first clogs she ever wore and he felt she was now of an age to value and treasure them. He told Louisa the story of how he acquired them.

In 1908 the caravan family was passing through Rochdale, the father walking the horse with one hand at its bridle, the other clasping the tiny hand of his youngest, barefoot child. Spotting a clog shop he rested his horse and paused to glance in the shop window before leading Louisa - not yet two - into the shop.

He requested a pair of clogs for his child, but after trying on the smallest sizes, the proprietor regretted he had not got a pair small enough.

"What about the little pair in the middle of your window?" asked her father. *"I'm sorry, sir"*, the man said, *"they are not for sale. They have been made specially as an advertisement for my business."*

"Try them on my child," said the father, with such a tone of insistence the proprietor felt bound to comply. Louisa's feet slid comfortably into the clogs.

"Name a fair price and I'll take them," said her father. The deal was struck and the clogs served Louisa well until the time she grew out of them. Her father had treasured them ever since.

In due course Alf Higginbotham came into Louisa's life and courted her, and with marriage in mind and the need of a home of her own she might well have left BWA at that point, but such was the regard in which she was held by her employers, a rule that only male workers could have tenancy of the company's properties was rescinded. Following the wedding, Louisa and Alf moved into 83 Arbourhay Street.

In 1950 came a move, again courtesy of BWA, to a comfy semi on Hurdsfield Estate where Louisa lived for more than 40 years before she went to the Trinity Home for the Elderly in the mid-1990s. Sadly, Louisa passed away on a weekend trip to Blackpool, in October 1997.

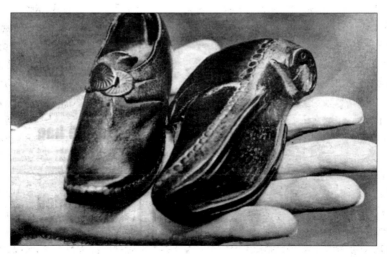

Louisa's Clogs resting on Geoffrey's hand.

22
The Big Lady

At some point in the mid 1990s, frustrated by the fact that for some months I had not had delivered to my home Macclesfield's Community News and was missing the articles of that treasure of a lady, Dorothy Bentley Smith, I took the trouble to cross town and call at their offices in Catherine Street, where they then were.

Back home with the current copy I found that on the Letters page a dispute was being waged as to whether the story of how our town became known as 'Treacle Town' was based on fact or fiction. There were letters 'for' and 'against' and such a debate surprised me; not only that, it saddened me and mildly irritated me.

Whether true or not the story of a large cask of treacle falling from a cart in Mill Street and being sufficiently damaged to permit the contents to flow freely and to allow the townsfolk to rush from their homes with their bowls, basins, etc. for their share of this God-given bounty has always seemed to me a charming tale from the past and one we should treasure as a rich fragment of our history. That the story has a genuine origin I have no doubt.

Some two or three years ago, Derek Ford, another local historian who has written some nice pieces in the past for the Old Macc magazine, paid me one of his occasional visits. Derek is always worth listening to and I asked him whether he had ever researched the legend of Treacle Town? Indeed he had. He believed the origin of the tale could well have been in the 1850s when a cask of spirits fell from a cart in town and a boy bystander imbibed so much of the released spirit - whether gin, whisky or rum I know not - that the lad died of alcoholic poisoning! The transition from spirit to treacle in the story, Derek suggested, came about with the passing of time.

Now it's my turn to get personally involved, for I have a story akin to the treacle one, which had similar legend potential, but where fate was foiled, in a manner of speaking.

During the war between 1943 and 1945 I was assistant storekeeper of Lonsdale and Adshead's wines and spirits department, Park Green, my immediate boss being Mr Ernest Lea. My main job was making up the wine and spirit orders for the brewery's public houses and the issue of Customs and Excise certificates.

Occasionally I would be asked to do a little bottling of the firm's own brand of wines and spirits.

What was not generally known was that the brewery had a property in Lowe Street, just a stone's throw away. This property was a small, nondescript, single storey, windowless building which had the appearance of being, perhaps, a one-man decorator's premises for storing his ladders and a few cans of paint.

Its small frontage was deceptive, for within, the small front room led into a much larger one which housed a stillage so thick-timbered and solid it could have withstood the weight of a large elephant without so much as a hint of the slightest creak. Upon the stillage sat a pipe of the finest port wine, recently tapped and ready to dispense its contents when called upon to do so.

A pipe was my favourite cask shape. Large, yes, with a capacity of 105 gallons, but the slenderest and most graceful of its ilk. I thought of her as The Big Lady and at that time she had surrendered little of her contents for she was a highly prized asset and drawn from frugally.

Mr Lea would say, maybe once every three months, *"Geoffrey, nip along to Lowe Street and take four bottles with you."* That was all that needed to be said. I would take four coloured bottles from our store and put them in a cardboard box together with four corks and a funnel, take the Lowe Street key off its hook and I was ready for my date with The Big Lady!

Inside the Lowe Street premises I would loosen the vent-peg (spigot) to allow smooth flow of the port, squat on an empty bottle crate, knees apart like a milkmaid, and fill the four bottles via the funnel. With the corks in place and the vent-peg inserted again tightly, I was ready to lock up and return to base. There I had a gadget, like a circular sponge-rubber vice, which allowed a tin-foil capsule to seal off the cork and upper neck of the bottle. The brewery's own label completed the job.

Well, one day I got the call again, something like ten weeks following my previous visit. I took the required number of bottles and accessories but found when I got there The Big Lady had started to leak. A hoop had loosened and there was seepage from between two staves, and a syrupy patch, four feet in diameter, glistened on the floor.

I hastened back to base and reported the crisis to Mr Lea who sent me posthaste to Mr Hyde, the cooper, to whom I transferred the key.

Of course it all ended happily. The Big Lady lived on. But it could so easily have been different with port wine and its rich aroma escaping in gallons under the front door, and Lowe Street residents with their bowls, basins, etc., rushing out of doors... Lowe Street might have been known as Port Wine Way today, and you can't say it wouldn't have had a genuine origin, can you?

23

Lower Hurdsfield and Those Streets of Yesteryear

Mr John Sutton of Symondley Road, Sutton, a close and respected friend, has furnished me with several interesting items pertaining to old Macclesfield during the years I have known him.

During the 1990s he delighted me by arranging for me to borrow several maps of the Macclesfield area dated 1874.

Naturally, I paid particular heed to the area of Lower Hurdsfield and the skein of streets nestling in the corner formed by Hurdsfield/Commercial Road and Buxton Road where I lived the early part of my life, with Arbourhay Street and Daybrook Street running parallel to each other and Waterloo Street at a right angle to them being the three longest in the complex.

Daybrook Street Boys' School was known as St. Luke's in those days and a few street names have also changed since those times.

Adelaide Street - synonymous with Sinnett's Fruit and Vegetable business throughout my years in the area - was Albert Street; the little cul-de-sac off Fence Street I knew as Welch Street (where Welchs' coal merchants had their stables) was William Street, and the Dicken Street I knew connecting Waterloo Street to Fence Street was Wellington Street. This latter change was surely predictable and desirable, for across town was a second Wellington Street - a short street, still extant - running parallel to Roe Street. I can well believe many a frustrated postman raised his glass of porter in support of that change!

Princess Street, Eastgate and Davies Street are clearly defined but the short cobbled link between Davies Street and Buxton Road, often referred to as the "Dunbar" is given the name Commongate. Nowhere is there any mention of the Dunbar.

The public house on Buxton Road almost opposite the Green Street opening is shown as the Brown Bull but the building which catches my eye, slightly lower down the road after the Commongate opening, is a large residence (equal in area to about six cottage homes) described as "The Hawthorns". Set back from Buxton Road, it had a front garden and was probably enclosed in railings with a gate access.

Behind this substantial building - that is to say, in the space between Eastgate and Davies Street, behind the Methodist Sunday School - was a large ornamental garden of shrubs with well-laid-out paths where residents and visitors could promenade at their leisure.

This charming place was not the unlikely oasis it might at first seem, for just a short distance east was the large area of open land destined to become Victoria Park in later years. This area, too, was tastefully trimmed with trees and shrubs.

The concealed garden of The Hawthorns brings me to another point. In my 1930s years living in Waterloo Street, I was aware of one or two "Courts" tucked away, but only because I had occasion to visit boyhood friends who lived in them. What this map has shown me is that the area was far more congested with homes and human life than I ever dreamed of. In my younger days we were not encouraged to investigate the abundance of ginnels, nor did there seem an incentive to do so.

So, how many Courts were there? Well, it is clear from the map that the space behind the house frontages of the established street network embracing King Street, Princess Street, Eastgate, Davies Street, York Street, Waterloo Street, Fence Street, Daybrook Street, Arbourhay and the little streets which crossed them, was fully utilised with more homes. Because these had to have identification, these areas were given court numbers and the houses they contained were numbered also. An address could, for example, be: Princess Street, Court No. 1, House No. 2, and so on.

In the relatively small area of land I have described, the number of clearly defined courts was 43! And I thought I knew that particular patch of the town. This congestion contrasts strongly with the site on the map of Hurdsfield House and its grounds, which is shown in glorious isolation in a large expanse of open country.

Incidentally, The Hawthorns at 49, Buxton Road was sited immediately behind where Arthur Watling had his motorcycle showroom in more recent times. My very obliging friend, John Sutton, is able to inform me further, thanks to his friends Dennis Whyte and Les Kirkham, that in 1881 The Hawthorns was the home of Mr Henry Boston, leather merchant, who was then aged 55. His sons were employed as shoemakers working on the premises.

Thank you, gentlemen, for that interesting and fitting conclusion.

24
A Slice of History

The name Richard Smith will not, I suspect, immediately bring to the minds of many Macclesfield folk a reminder of an illustrious past, and yet our town and indeed, our nation, owes a very great deal to this gentleman.

In or about the year 1885, Mr Smith, who came from Stone in Staffordshire had, quite literally, a germ of an idea. His interest was in the milling of flour and a puzzling feature of it. It was generally accepted by millers at the time that although wheat germ contained most of the nutrients, it had to be discarded in the milling process because, with its inclusion, flour tended to sour quickly. The special vitalizing and nourishing qualities of the living germ were little understood in those days but Smith realised that this vital ingredient, hitherto relegated to pig food could, if properly treated, be returned to the flour. His experiments in steaming the wheatgerm to stabilise it were successful and Smith's patent Germ Flour came in to being.

Astute as he had been so far he recognised that he lacked the business accumen to match his invention and he approached Macclesfield miller Thomas Cliffe Fitton who agreed to market the flour commencing in 1886.

The enterprise did not meet with much enthusiasm at the outset. Bakers, confectioners, and the public were suspicious of the product. The word 'germ' for example was an off-putting element to sales of the bread and so, three years after its launch, Smith and Fitton organised a national competition to find a new name.

The competition was won by a London student named Herbert Grime who suggested the name Hovis. His idea, he explained, was constructed from the Latin words Hominus Vis, meaning 'the strength of man.' He had placed a circumflex (a ripple stroke) over the 'O' indicating the omitted Latin letters; this was dropped some years later.

For his effort Mr Grime received £25. Many years later his widow was given a pension in acknowledgement of the company's long term gratitude.

It was at this time also that John Figgins Morton arrived on the scene. A youth of 18, he joined the company to build up the Sales Department. A firm believer in advertising, his promotional expertise was ably supported by Mr A.E. Cressall, who pursued with unflagging zeal the medical and scientific value of Hovis bread with the medical profession and press, and ensured that what had been an ailing infant began to grow, thrive and flourish. In the first year, in which Mr Morton was responsible for all the advertising and business side, winning the goodwill of the baking trade, and control of the quality and consistency of flour production, the company showed a profit of £26,000.

Advertising was the name of the game. The Hovis Company advertised on everything and in everything with the constant emphasis on the good health-producing virtues of their bread. The public was assured that Hovis formed 'good bone, brain, flesh and muscle.' In the early days the company sold only flour and supplied tins embossed with the Hovis name to bakers, but thanks to spreading fame - which Queen Victoria and the royal family did much to enhance - the business grew and grew. Progressively, then, the company took over bakers and began selling their own bread.

Through the years competitions for improving the quality of baking bread, cakes and bakers' sundries were organised between master bakers and valuable prizes were offered. Hovis certificates were much sought-after trophies by those in the trade.

In 1906 Hovis ran a verse competition in the Daily Mail with a £5 first

'*Hovis every Day*'—
The first Rule of Health

HOVIS LTD., LONDON, MACCLESFIELD, BRISTOL, Etc.

prize and £3 for second. Canon Frederick Langridge of Limerick won the fiver for this gem of an entry.

>Who's the girl a man should wed?
>One like Hovis, honest bred,
>Full of energy and tone,
>With a sweetness all her own:
>Never prone to disagree,
>Flower of perfect purity!

In 1910 the flour-milling machinery was moved to Manchester and the whole of the Macclesfield building turned over to the Printing Department. Through the ensuing years the company built up valuable ancillary services which developed into important businesses on their own accounts. Van building, garage and depot businesses throughout the land, sign work, letter making, painting and guilding for advertisement purposes, bakers' signs, bag-making etc.

Signs announcing 'Teas with Hovis' sprang up everywhere, and the name became a household word. 'Don't say brown say Hovis' is probably the best remembered slogan of all. Today output is several million loaves each week with a choice on offer of wholemeal, the most popular stone-ground wholemeal, oatbran, Hovis granary country grain wholemeal, organic and the old original wheatgerm.

Mr Richard Smith, the originator of Hovis did not live long enough to see the results of his work; he died in 1900. Mr J.F. Morton prospered and eventually retired as chairman of the company in 1957, and today, although this greatly respected gentleman is no longer with us, his name continues to be perpetuated with the Morton Hall in Union Road, built in 1939.

Wary of imitators, the Hovis Company guarded their product and its good name jealously. 'Merciless' would not be too strong an adjective to describe the action taken against those who sought, spuriously, to benefit from its reputation, and in the early years, particularly, courts were kept busy dealing with offenders.

On a personal note, I recall an incident on Christmas Eve in 1941 when I was employed as a baker's boy by Mr Arthur Cox, of South Street, off Byron Street. Early in the day he said, *"Take the big bike, Geoffrey, and go to Mr Coppenhall's. He's expecting you and is giving us a loan of some tins to help us out."* The big bike was the one with the big basket on the front and within minutes I was at Mr Roland Coppenhall's bakehouse, just below the Bank

The Macclesfield Hovis Mill in the late 1940s.

Street turning. Since the baking tins fitted inside each other I returned to South Street with a fair load.

Both Mr Cox and Mr Coppenhall were renowned for their products. I was never to witness Mr Coppenhall's dexterity but Mr Cox was an absolute genius handling the dough, whether it be one large portion getting the firm symmetrical treatment with the rhythm of both hands or separate smaller portions in each hand.

Anyway, with the pressure of extra baking an error was made and some time later we discovered that a batch of small Hovis loaves had been baked in plain tins and emerged from the oven without identity, whereas the small fruit loaves were proudly displaying 'Hovis' on their sides. I regarded the mix-up with undisguised hilarity at first, but Mr Cox was quick to suppress my humour and pointed out that a serious breech of the Hovis code had been made. *"Hovis bread,"* he said, *"should have the name written on it, and Hovis tins should have nothing baked in them but a Hovis mix!"* We were therefore guilty on two counts.

It is to Mr Cox's credit that he was deeply concerned but, in the end we had to take a chance. I was not to bring the matter to the notice of anyone on my delivery rounds and we could only hope that hearty appetites over the next few days would remove all evidence of default. And so it proved...

Derby Street, off Mill Street, with New Day Furnishing stores on the right ...

... and Ashton sports outfitters on the left, where the street has turned to join Chestergate.

25
The Kindness that was Old Macclesfield

One afternoon in 2000, I received a phone call from my good friend Keith Mason of Byrons Lane. That day his business had taken him to Fence House, one of the Alms-houses on Buxton Road.

"They have a really interesting tablet on an inside wall there, dated 1889. I think you should see it and I've told the people there that you'll probably be paying them a visit soon and they'll be happy to see you."

I thanked Keith for his staunch support of Old Macc, for which I was local agent.

"Incidentally," he added, *"Fence house is the Alms-house with its back overlooking the first part of Green Street, and did you know that at one time it was a hospital? That is what the tablet says."*

Given that information, I delved into my old maps. A 1909 edition showing the Alms-houses had no reference to a hospital but a Business Street Map of the town, undated but believed by me to have been published about 1896, had it clearly marked.

The next morning I took Keith's advice and strolled down Buxton Road from where I had joined it at Flint Street, eager to learn something new. As I turned left and passed through the gateway into the quadrangle of Fence Court I was, as ever, awed by the splendour of these buildings with their fine stock-brick exteriors and Elizabethan-style gables, still in fine fettle in their second century of existence. High up, in the centre, was this description:

T.U.B. Fence Alms-Houses F.D.B. 1895

The initials are a reference to two Brocklehurst brothers; but more about them later.

At Fence House I made myself known to a lady secretary, Mrs Anita Hall, who greeted me warmly and explained that the premises were from where Mrs Heather Jobling and Company, Solicitors, conducted their business. With original panelling still to be seen the sense of history was palpable and I felt greatly privileged to be there. I had two further appointments that morning so my main concern was the tablet which had excited Keith the previous day. It was of brass and bore this text:

FENCE HOSPITAL

Where this building stands, a poor crippled girl lived with her bedridden mother whom she supported. She could move only on crutches, and during the many years of her work at the Old Silk Mill in Hurdsfield Road her companions used to help her on her way on dark winter mornings. When the mother died the daughter said her own strength was gone and her work in life done. She took to her bed without a murmur and lived only a few days more.

The founder of this Hospital during his life expressed his wish that her lowly life of filial duty should be commemorated on the spot which it had hallowed, and that hereafter among the Spirits made perfect, he might come to know her. In fulfilment of the former desire this tablet is erected. A.D. 1889.

I declined, with thanks, Mrs Hall's offer to inspect the premises further at that point and with a promise to return at a later date, I took my leave.

There were two questions posed by the tablet. Firstly, the term 'hospital'. Although Fence House was comfortably spacious in a homely sense, it seemed to be too insubstantial in size to merit the term 'hospital' as most people understand the word and, secondly, just who was the poor cripple whose dedication to her mother and employer had earned such a tribute?

I reckoned there was a reasonable chance that on whatever day in 1889 the tablet had been dedicated, the local press would have been invited to attend, and if so, would have contributed more information on the subject.

That afternoon I visited the

Wall plaque depicting Macclesfield's proud silk heritage.

Fence House, formerly Fence Hospital.

reference department of Macclesfield Public Library and was lucky to obtain an hour's immediate study, on film, of the Macclesfield Courier and Herald for that year.

Of necessity, my inspection of 52 editions of the newspaper was cursory, but almost immediately I enjoyed astonishing good fortune, for written within the January pages I came across this illuminating report:

'**FENCE HOSPITAL:** *This useful institution continues in a quiet and unostentatious manner to do its work on the lines lain down by its founder, the late Thomas Unett Brocklehurst, Esq., of Henbury Park. The object of the institution is to provide, in the dining hall of the hospital, good meat dinners to those work people of Macclesfield who, after recovering from illness, need strengthening food as may establish their health and enable them to return to work with as little delay as possible. During the year just passed 404 convalescent patients have benefited from this provision of nourishing food, and no less that 2,424 dinners, consisting of roast meat, bread, potatoes, pudding and milk have been served and presided over by the matron, Mrs Bailey, with the utmost regard to cleanliness, comfort and order. Dinner tickets for distribution may be had on application to Mrs Fell, at Henbury Park, Macclesfield. Each ticket entitles the recipient to a course of six dinners.'*

This report was followed by a list of those who had received tickets distributed during that year by the doctors and ladies of the town and neighbourhood and was probably dictated by propriety, and to show evidence of precise expenditure, but whether recipients of this charity appreciated being named in this way is questionable, I would have thought.

The 'hospital' description was now explained, the word being used in its more archaic sense, meaning 'a charitable home', a true Alms-house in fact. My continued trawl through the rest of that year's news provided nothing relating to the poor cripple and the brass tablet, but I considered myself amply rewarded for my trouble.

I made an appointment with solicitor Mrs Jobling to visit Fence House again, a week later. Mrs Jobling very kindly conducted my tour of the house herself and I was permitted to take a few photographs. A few structural changes have been made through the years but my impression of the ground floor was that originally it had been, principally, a single hall, supporting my theory that the premises had been built with the charitable function always in mind.

Panelled stairway at Fence House.

It was a considerable treat for me to climb the dark, glistening, panelled staircase and to see, in Mrs Jobling's own office, high on the wall on each side of the window, a plaque depicting, in relief, the Brocklehurst family's link with the silk industry. The first plaque is a representation of a silk worm, cocoon and moth, encircled by mulberry leaves and berries. The second plaque depicts a silk weaver busy at the loom.

To conclude, I feel it will be appropriate to reflect on the 'Fence' branch of the Brocklehurst family. In 1896 Mr Thomas Brocklehurst, one of the founders of the great silk firm of Messrs J & T Brocklehurst and of the highly esteemed Brocklehurst's Bank, purchased from the Smyth family the original Fence House, which was a fine old mansion situated in the centre of what is now the Buxton Road section of Victoria Park. He had three sons: Charles, Thomas Unett and Francis Dicken Brocklehurst.

On the death of the father, Fence House and the estate passed down to Charles, but in 1884 both Charles and his brother, Thomas Unett, died within a short time of each other and Francis Dicken Brocklehurst came into possession. It was he, who, in 1894 - one year before the Alms-houses were completed - presented the estate to the borough. Fence House was taken down and the estate converted into a public park and recreation area.

This generous gentleman passed away in 1905 and in 1908 a granite pillar was erected in Victoria Park on the site of the ancestral home to commemorate his many acts of kindness and gifts to the Town. It stands there to this day.

26
A Tragedy Offstage

The lack of cinema in Macclesfield today is a subject of much criticism and speculation and it is interesting to note that a similar deficiency existed in the late 1890s when live theatre ceased for a time in the town.

The Theatre Royal, Mill Street, which was on the site of where Duke's Court is today and where the Salvation Army Citadel was located before that, had opened in 1811 and served the town until its closure in 1875. The void created after this long sequence of theatrical activity lasted until 1883 when the New Theatre Royal & Opera House was built and opened in Catherine Street. It was destined not to rival the longevity of the earlier theatre as it ended its existence in flames on Easter Saturday, April 4th, 1931.

The theatre's shocking and tragic ending accepted, one of the saddest stories associated with its existence occurred early in 1889, just as the new year had got into its stride. Patrons had savoured Mr W. H. Hallatt and "His Powerful and Dramatic Company" portraying *Is Life Worth Living?* which starred talented actress Miss Lyton. Mr P. Mullholland and his Celebrated

Company had presented the great drama 'Mizpah'.

Macclesfield favourite Mr Walter Casson, supported by another 'Powerful Company' had staged the new and original comedy-drama entitled *My Playmate,* and one week later Mr R. Morand featured the Great Drama, *Mother's Sin*, a title highly suited to the Victorian age with its rich promise of pathos.

Messrs Glovers & Grundy had featured in the latest London success 'Arabian Nights' and in its wake came the Grand Pantomime 'Sinbad the Sailor' which had a 'Grand transformation' scene painted by E. J. Davis.

Which brings me to the sad story I have mentioned....

On Monday evening February 25th, the theatre's thespian offering was 'Eviction' which was very much a family production in that it was presented by Mr Hubert O'Grady and the small cast included Frank O'Grady and his wife Isabella. The O'Grady family emanated from Dublin.

Each time 33 year old Isabella exited the stage, as per script, she returned to the dressing room, took her seat, picked up her knitting from the table in front her of her and passed the brief periods in this way. At 9.30 she was similarly employed when actress Susannah Willie joined her in the dressing room. For whatever reason - perhaps a costume change - Miss Willie found it necessary to pass backwards and forwards behind Mrs O'Grady, and since space was limited the knitter would lean forward each time this occurred. On one of these occasions one of Mrs O'Grady's knitting needles caught on the edge of the table resulting in a penetration of her breast..

It would seem that the offending needle was of steel and sharpened at each end - it is likely that the actress was knitting socks for her husband which would require four such needles. She immediately reported the accident to Miss Willie and complained of pain and discomfort and Miss Willie witnessed the little blood that was visible. Unfortunately the actresses were recalled to the stage almost immediately. Mrs O'Grady found it difficult to play her part and felt faint but suffered the ordeal to the play's end.

At about 10.45 Miss Willie accompanied her home to her digs at 8 Little Street where her husband joined her shortly afterwards. In an aside to the husband Miss Willie offered the opinion that his wife had frightened herself more than was necessary - no doubt based on the apparently superficial wound she had seen.

As the poor lady's distress intensified, at 3am surgeon Mr Wigmore was sent for and he diagnosed a punctured lung. Subsequently, during the next two days she was attended by Mr Somerville of Park Street and a Mr Fernie but died at 6 o'clock on the Thursday morning.

During my research for this article I discussed this case with a doctor friend of mine and I acknowledge here my gratitude for his comments. Having listened to the story, he felt able to speak confidently on the case. Put simply this unfortunate lady had sustained a peripheral puncture to the heart, causing a slow and constant loss of blood resulting in her death. It would not happen today, he said. The patient would be scanned, the damage accurately sited and the operation would be a formality.

The inquest on Isabella O'Grady was held at the Town Hall, Macclesfield, on the afternoon of her death. Mr Fred H.Wigmore, surgeon, gave the cause death as penetration of the lung. From the first, he said, he thought her chances of recovery remote. He did not think that if he had been called in at once he could have done much to save her. A verdict of Accidental Death was returned.

27

A Town in Mourning

Young widow and mother Emily Halton felt a great sense of unease in her house at 60 Fence Street that Saturday morning as the hands of her clock came together for 12 noon. Her only child, eight-years-old daughter Mary Ann, should have been home by then. She had left the house an hour and a half earlier to collect her mother's weekly wage from Bamford's silk mill, Waller Street, Sutton. Wearing a new straw hat and with her mother's purse tucked in her dress pocket, she had assured her mum she would be back within the hour and was a reliable child.

With the recent loss of her husband, Emily Hatton had to work long hours as a spinner for the 12s 3d weekly wage but on that March 24th day of 1877, as more time passed without sight of her daughter, it was concern for her child that was uppermost in her mind.

At 2pm Mrs Halton put on her coat and took the route she knew her daughter would have taken, and reached the Sutton factory without any sign of her. She explained her concern to the manager, Mr Robinson. Yes, he told her, Mary Ann had collected her wages that morning at about 10-50; she had counted the money carefully and placed it in her mother's purse and pocketed it for safety. There was something odd, though, he told Emily. Half an hour before Mary Ann had arrived a local lad, Sam Goodwin, had come to the factory with a note purporting to be from Mrs Halton, asking that the bearer be given her wages as her daughter was sick. The manager, knowing that Mrs Halton could neither read nor write, had refused the request.

Mrs Halton quickly found where young Goodwin lived close by and he told her that just after 10 o'clock he and his two pals were approached by a man as they stood in Mill Lane at the corner of Waller Street. The man, who was carrying a brown basket, asked Goodwin to take the note to the mill manager. On the boy's return without the money the man had hurried away disappointed.

The boy described the man as young, stunted in growth and dwarf-like in appearance. This matched the description of Harry Leigh, 23-years-old stepson of Mrs Halton's next-door neighbour, Mrs Ann Leigh. What's more, Mrs Halton remembered that Harry Leigh - recently married and living in Parsonage Street -had been present the day before when she had discussed Mary Ann's errand duty with her neighbour.

Mrs Halton hastened to Leigh's home in Parsonage Street, told him of her concern for her missing daughter and that she was positive that he had attempted to obtain her wages with a forged note. Leigh claimed that the whole story was a complete mystery to him. Mrs Halton threatened to report the facts to the police. Leigh advised her to do so.

At the police station in Churchside the sergeant listened sympathetically and Mrs Halton was informed gently that the body of an unidentified young girl had been taken from the canal near Hollins bridge a few hours earlier by a passing blacksmith, Joe Jackson. He had taken the body to the Railway View Inn and it was now lying in the mortuary close by. Mrs Halton was spared the information that the body had been still warm when removed from the water but warned that she would be required to view the body and that there was some damage to the child's face.

Mrs Halton formally identified her daughter's body. The pocket of her child's dress that had contained the purse had been torn away. A brown basket found on the canal tow-path was shown to her as well but she had never seen it before. Following this distressing duty Mrs Halton divulged her suspicions of Harry Leigh to the police.

At 5 pm Inspector Swindells led officers to Leigh's home to find he had barricaded himself in the outside privy and refused to come out. Questioned through the locked door Leigh again claimed no knowledge of the little girl's disappearance or of the forged note. Told that the child had been found dead he claimed he had been working that morning at Briar's Mill, Bollington. At that the Inspector took his leave to confirm Leigh's story. Arriving at the mill in Bollington he was assured by the foreman that Leigh, normally employed there as a weaver, had not been in work for a fortnight.

The Inspector and his men returned to Parsonage Street to find Leigh still locked in the privy. Leigh's wife maintained that her husband had left the house each morning as if leaving for work and had given her eight shillings that very afternoon.

Inspector Swindells ordered his men to break down the privy door and Leigh was taken into custody, searched, and found to have a copper or two on his person. Police found a further 3s 9d concealed in the house and these sums and Leigh's expenses for beer on that day, confirmed later, totalled an incriminating 12s 3d, the precise figure of Mrs Halton's wage!

Charged with Mary Ann's murder, Leigh maintained his claim of innocence. The boy, Sam Goodwin, and his two pals identified Leigh as the man with the forged note. Four more witnesses came forward who had seen Mary Ann accompanied by a little man that morning, one of whom - Emma Owen, a servant girl - claimed to have seen Leigh actually on the canal towpath swinging a basket with a young girl wearing a straw hat. All four identified Leigh as the man in question.

The puzzle of the basket's real owner was soon resolved. Charlie Wright, an 11-year-old schoolboy from Bollington came forward and identified the basket as his, for his mother had repaired the lid with copper wire. He had absent-mindedly left the basket on a form at Bollington station on his way to school at Macclesfield. It had contained a custard tart that he was taking to his aunt. When found at the canal-side the tart had gone but several pencils were found in it. A pencil holder found on Leigh was identified by Mrs Halton as belonging to her daughter.

On March 28th the whole town turned out for Mary Ann's funeral as her coffin was conveyed to Macclesfield Cemetery. A few days later the Mayor launched an appeal fund for the mother, and the townsfolk responded generously.

In his police cell on March 31st Leigh made an attempt on his own life by fashioning a noose from a silk handkerchief. He was thwarted just in time. On April 3rd he volunteered a new statement and admitted not going in to work on that fatal day. He now claimed to have had an early drinking session at the Spinners' Arms, Bollington, followed by an early afternoon visit to the Ship Inn, Beech Lane, before returning home for his dinner, thereby accounting for all his time before his arrest.

His Bollington pub visit was disputed by the landlord, Levi Brown, and by a customer who Leigh claimed to have seen. The landlady of the Ship Inn confirmed Leigh's visit at about 1 pm. He had claimed to her then that he had walked from Bollington and looked pale and agitated, she added.

On Saturday, April 7th, Harry Leigh was brought before the magistrates and charged with murder and attempted suicide. He admitted the suicide attempt but insisted his innocence in respect of the child's death.

Committed for trial at Chester Assizes, he appeared before Mr Baron Bramwell on July 24th, 1877, pleading "not guilty". With so overwhelming a case against him his defending counsel, Mr Burke Wood, sought to reduce the charge from murder to manslaughter claiming the child had run to her death in the canal in attempting to escape from Leigh, but the medical evidence concluded that her bruised and scratched face was consistent with her having been gripped tightly about the mouth. The tops of her arms were badly bruised also, but there was no suggestion of sexual assault.

The jury retired and returned with a guilty verdict 25 minutes later and the judge concurred with its decision. Leigh was sentenced to death. In Chester Castle, awaiting execution, he finally showed remorse and admitted throwing Mary Ann into the canal after robbing her, and leaving her to drown. He wrote to Mrs Halton, pleading for her forgiveness. Through a letter written for her by a clergyman, she did so.

Despite his congenital handicap of stunted growth, Leigh, it appears, was an intelligent man who had received a good education. He had held the position of assistant to the Borough Surveyor but had thrown in his job in a fit of pique following a dispute over wages. Because of his lack of appetite for work that he considered to be beneath him his life went into decline. It was finally terminated by hangman William Marwood at Chester Castle on August 13th, 1877.

28
Days of the Puffing Billy

Considering that the first public steam line, the Stockton and Darlington Railway, was opened in 1825 and the first inter-city railway, the Liverpool and Manchester line, was opened five years later, one is bound to conclude that Macclesfield was well-served in achieving railway communication with Stockport and Manchester by 1845. By 1837 a mere 1,500 miles of track were laid in the UK- in the following 50 years this figure was increased eleven-fold; statistics that endorse our town's good fortune.

Railways were, in those times, an exciting business. For those locals able to afford the four pence ha'penny for a copy of the Macclesfield Courier and Herald the progress of the railway system was usually the main news topic.

Macclesfield's first railway station was situated near Beech Lane bridge and the 1845 opening of the railway line was an event of supreme importance with thousands of people making their way to Beech Lane and lining the railway embankment to witness the first 'Puffing Billy' to leave the station on its journey to Manchester. In total 180 people were invited to be passengers on that auspicious occasion. Dignitaries included the Chairman, Mr Joshua Proctor, who was Chief Director of the Railway Company; the Mayor (Mr George Wright) and Mr John Brocklehurst, MP

Having reached Manchester this large party paused briefly before returning to Macclesfield where a vast concourse of people awaited them, including a brass band to accompany the triumphant party from Beech Lane to the Town Hall for a sumptuous banquet.

Local schoolmaster and historian John Earles, recalling the event in 1915, had this to say of the train's homecoming:

In introducing the Chairman, Mr John Brocklehurst said that it was the first time that the Mayor and Corporation of Macclesfield had ventured on a journey of twenty miles from home and returned the same day in safety.

Sir Wm. Thompson, in a racy speech, quoted from an oration which was delivered in the House of Commons in the year 1671, wherein the speaker said: "Sir, if a man were to come to this House and tell us that he

Joe Forrest Jnr on one of the cannons at West Park.

was to convey us to Edinburgh in coaches in seven days, should we not vote him to Bedlam? Surely we should if we did him justice. Or if another told us that he would carry us to the Indies in six months, should we not punish him for practising on our credulity?" And yet the good people of Macclesfield had that day seen a train depart from Beech Lane and convey 180 people to Manchester in an hour and bring them back in the same time.

The Beech Lane station was not to be used for long. The Beech Lane Tunnel was completed and opened for traffic in 1849 and a new railway station was constructed in Hibel Road.

In 1852 an idea was mooted to convert the Town Field, situated in what was then called Prestbury Lane in the north-west outskirts of the town, into a Public Park. The Town Field had for many years been used for public meetings and military training. This early speculation bore fruit quickly and in 1854 the Public Park - West Park, as we now know it - was duly opened, thanks in no small way, to the contributions of the town's workers, in much the same way that the building of Macclesfield Infirmary would be funded 25 years later.

On that 4th day of October when the opening of the park was celebrated, Britain and her ally, France, had been at war with Russia for six months in support of Turkey, and the Crimean War, caused by Russia's expansionist ambitions in the Balkans, was to continue for another year and a half. Curiously, this conflict, which resulted in the loss of half a million lives (mainly from cholera and typhus), became linked to West Park and Hibel Road railway station by an event in June 1857.

After the Black Sea port of Sebastopol capitulated to Allied forces following a year long siege in September 1855, peace was achieved early in 1856. The Russian cannons used in the defence of Sebastopol immediately became desirable trophies of war and Macclesfield Corporation, with the support of the Marquis of Westminster, applied to be considered.

Queen Victoria, it is said, expressly stated that Macclesfield was not to be overlooked when such trophies were allocated. Perhaps Her Majesty retained fond memories of resting at the Macclesfield Arms on 18th October, 1832, when as Princess Victoria, she and her mother, the Duchess of Kent, journeyed from Eaton Hall, Chester, to Chatsworth House, Derbyshire.

Be that as it may, Macclesfield was awarded two cannons and these were later complemented by original mountings and gun carriages, and Wednesday 24th June, 1857 was chosen for the ceremony of transferring the guns to the Public Park from Hibel Road station. In the event it proved to be a double celebration....

A prominent citizen of those times, Mr Joseph Hudson Beswick, had, buried deep in his field at Oxford Road, a large Boulder Stone weighing an estimated 30 tons. This rock, unconnected with the geology of this area and believed to be a relic of the Ice Age was offered to the Corporation, and Mr Aspinwall, the borough surveyor, supervised the disinterment of this giant mass prior to its removal to the Public Park on the same day as the cannons. The cannons, each believed capable of firing a 42 pounder ball, were bronzed and painted to remedy their worn look.

The weather on the day was scorching and many protected themselves with umbrellas. The Mayor, members of the Corporation and other gentlemen who intended to form part of the procession assembled in the new vestibule of the Town Hall at 2pm before making their way to Hibel Road . In attendance also were the Macclesfield Brass Band, a drum and fife band and a military band. The guns, towards the end of the procession, were drawn by eight horses followed by Crimean Veterans, pensioners and the Cheshire Yeomanry. They journeyed to the park via Waters Green, Sunderland Street, Mill Street, Chestergate and Prestbury Lane where the horses were unharnessed and sent to collect Mr Beswick's ponderous gift whilst the dignitaries refreshed themselves.

According to Mr Isaac Finney, bookseller of Chestergate, in his book *Antiquities of Old Macclesfield* published in 1871, several more horses were needed to convey the huge boulder on the wagon (which itself weighed $5\frac{1}{2}$ tons) to its situation in the park. The Boulder Stone is still to be seen in the West Park but the two Russian cannons were surrendered to the 1939-45 war effort, together with many other metal things that are sadly missed.

29
Macclesfield Borough Police 1836-1947

The date 19th January, 1836, was a most important one in our town's history. On that date the Borough Police Force was inaugurated and William Lockett was appointed the first Chief Constable.

Five days earlier, the first Watch Committee had been appointed and comprised His Worship the Mayor, Samuel Thorp, Jeremiah Clark, Charles Corbishley, Richard Wych, John Stansfield, Thomas Airey and Thomas Jackson.

As has been shown, the Watch Committee wasted no time stamping its seal on the new regime and resolved:

That the Chief Constable have six efficient constables, four for the day and two for the night, the day constables to take it in turns to be on duty with the night police and that the Chief Constable have the assistance of four special constables for Saturday nights and Sundays.

The uniform consisted of tall hats with long silk fur, the crown of the hat being covered with a patent leather, a narrow strip of the same material down either side, double-breasted swallow coat tails and white trousers. The style of this uniform followed very closely that adopted by Sir Robert Peel's first Metropolitan Police Force.

Prior to the passing of the Municipal Corporations Act, 1835, law and order had been the responsibility of what were termed "Charleys". "Charleys" were stationed in watch boxes at various centres throughout the town and used to carry large sticks with horn lanterns lighted with candles. In addition, at times of public disturbance, there were volunteer nightly patrols, their numbers embodied by all the respectable householders of the town and neighbourhood, irrespective of their profession or relative social position. They were the forerunners of today's Special Constabulary.

To its credit, the early Force kept some form of records and a perusal of the very first Charge Book and the punishments meted out, will raise a few eye-brows today.

The use of the stocks as punishment had been long established and continued to be frequently applied. The extract from Isaac Finney's *Macklesfelde in Ye Olden Time* is most informative:

"In many places the stocks were often so constructed as to serve both stocks and whipping posts, the posts which supported the stocks being made sufficiently high were furnished near the top with iron clasps to fasten round the wrists of offenders, and hold them securely during the infliction of the punishment. The stocks formerly used at Macclesfield were not so constructed. The plan adopted when a case of whipping or flogging occurred was to make use of the top of the steps leading into the Old Town Hall where the culprit (male or female, for both sexes were whipped) was

Date	Charge	Sentence
22 January, 1843	Youth aged 19 years. Burglary	Transported 10 years
30 January, 1843	Youth aged 17 years, suspicion of breaking into slaughter house and stealing 50 lbs. pork and one sack	Transported 7 years
16 February, 1843	Man aged 24 years, stealing pair of Quarter boots	Transported 7 years
27 February, 1843	Youth aged 19 years, stealing a silver watch, 3 blankets and a silver caddy spoon	Transported 7 years
9 July, 1843	Man aged 43 years, drunk and disorderly	Fined 5 shillings and se in stocks
11 July, 1843	Man 27 years, stealing 4 sacks, pair of trousers, velveteen jacket and quantity of horse hair	Transported 7 years
22 July, 1843	Two boys (each aged 11, stealing a rabbit	14 days each and to be whipped on the 7th day

secured to the railing prior to the infliction of the punishment, so that the iron rails served both for this purpose and also for hanging, as for example, the man or deserter who was hung from them at the time when the Duke of Cumberland passed through the town in 1745 in pursuit of Prince Charles Edward Stuart."

The last case of whipping in Macclesfield occurred about the year 1831 when a young man was publicly whipped in front of the Town Hall.

"In attending to the old stocks, we may well remark that after their demolition in the year 1828, new ones were made of iron and placed under the balcony of the New Town Hall, and were occasionally used: but after a short time they were also dispensed with and put by as lumber so that now the punishment is altogether abolished."

Another form of punishment was the ducking stool-girdle. The Macclesfield appliance is understood to have been in use in a pit now occupied by Central Station, and the street Cuckstoolpit Hill, is said to be named in consequence and may well have afforded a tiered vantage point for spectators to witness the ducking of scolding women in the pit. The words ducking and cucking would seem to be synonymous.

The fledgling Police Force increased in size through the years and in 1875 a year after Mr William Sheasby was appointed Chief Constable, it was increased from one Chief Constable, four sergeants and thirteen constables to one Chief Constable, two inspectors, five sergeants and twenty-eight constables, and a superannuation fund was established. Police duties were obviously on the increase, as two years later two further constables were added to the authorised establishment.

Mr Sheasby remained in office as Chief Constable for 29 years, resigning his post on Christmas Day, 1903.

He could consider himself lucky for having survived for so long. Early in 1882 an attempt was made on his life. Mr Sheasby was walking in Great King Street, where he lived, when he was attacked by a man with a knife who had been lying in wait at the corner of Catherine Street. Mr Sheasby sustained serious injury and at the Cheshire Assizes the man concerned was sentenced to penal servitude for life.

In 1907 Mr Sheasby's son was appointed Chief Constable and served the town in that capacity for 34 years, retiring in 1942. The combined service

The Macclesfield Constabulary 1946. This group photograph would have included the Hurdsfield 'Bobbies': PCs Bailey, Johnson and Greenall, all residing in Brocklehurst Avenue and, just a stone's throw away, Inspector Frank Dent, whose home was on The Crescent

of William and Henry Sheasby as Chief Constables was 64 years.

A surprising item from Borough Police records is that in 1849 the police cells were heated with hot water. This conflicts with the Spartan conditions one would expect, but it must have been a boon to the vagrants of those times.

Other items offer a quaint comparison to the technological world in which we wallow today. In 1888 the Police Station had its first telephone installed via the Macclesfield and Bollington section of Lancashire and Cheshire Telephone Company. In 1889 an electric bell was fitted in the house of the Captain of the Volunteer Fire Brigade, connected with the Police Station. A year later, a further telephone linked the Station to the Corporation Fire Brigade. That same year the police were supplied with a "Typograph" (ie duplicator) obtained at a cost of 45 shillings. In 1909 a first typewriter was purchased for police use and in 1905 two bicycles were purchased to increase their efficiency.

Following the Great War the Desborough Committee was appointed to improve conditions in the Police Service and, to its credit, succeeded in achieving its goal. It also commenced the merger of the smaller Police Forces, a move that Macclesfield Borough Police Force resisted. Amalgamation was in the air again in 1931/32 and the local Watch Committee took appropriate action to oppose the proposal.

However, at midnight on the 31st March, 1947, the Borough Police Force became part of the Cheshire Constabulary, Inspector F.H. Dent being the very last officer to retire from the Macclesfield Police Force.

30
The Audacious Mr Wakefield

Edward Gibbon Wakefield, born on 20th March 1796, was the eldest of four sons of Edward Wakefield and his wife Susanna, his brothers being Arthur, William Hayward and Felix, each of them born three or four years apart. Edward Gibbon was educated at Westminster School between 1808 and 1810 and at Edinburgh High School, finally leaving in 1812.

Although he had found fault with both teaching institutions, by all accounts he had developed into a young man of great ability and personal attraction, and on the threshold of employment none could have foreseen that he was destined to perpetrate a crime that would send shock waves throughout the country, emanating from the picturesque area of Cheshire in which we live.

In 1814, thanks to his father's influence, Edward entered the employment of William Hill, envoy to the court of Turin. In 1816 he eloped with an heiress, Eliza Susan Pattle, the orphan daughter of a Canton merchant. He afterwards returned to Turin as secretary to the under-secretary of the legation, and after his wife's death in 1820 he became connected with the Paris legation. He was, by then, father to Edward Jerningham and Susan Priscilla.

It is likely that the Wakefield family's first link with Macclesfield was formed when father Edward, widowed for some years, married in Paris in 1822, without her father's knowledge, Miss Frances Davis, a lady much his junior in years, her father being Dr David Davis, headmaster of Macclesfield Grammar School.

It is the events of 1826 upon which we must focus particular attention. In February of that year Edward Gibbon Wakefield and his brother William visited Macclesfield. That Edward considered himself in straightened circumstances and sought means to improve his lot there can be no doubt; but what was the cause? Local historian John Earles writing of these events early last century claims that Edward had exhausted his means by leading a life of pleasure in the French capital. This may be so, but I have found no evidence to support this view. That he had two small children and employed a governess and a manservant must not be forgotten.

Be that as it may, he came to Macclesfield and brought his troubles with him and confided his concerns to his stepmother who was of a similar age to himself, which goes some way to explain the affinity they established.

To his stepmother - Fanny, as she was known - was attributed the idea that Edward's remarriage to a wealthy heiress could solve all his problems; and what is more, a young lady fitting the bill was relatively close at hand.

Mr William Turner of Shrigley Hall, Pott Shrigley, was a wealthy manufacturer and High Sheriff of Cheshire. He had a daughter Ellen, just 15, a young lady described as having a lively disposition, quick perception and personal beauty. Miss Turner had for some time been educated at the school of a Mrs Daulby in Liverpool.

A plot was hatched by Edward, his brother William and their stepmother to abduct Ellen Turner and to trick her into marriage with Edward Wakefield and thereby secure his future. Accordingly, on the evening of 5th March, 1826, the two brothers took their leave of Macclesfield with the professed object of proceeding to London on their way to Paris. But instead of taking that road, at seven o'clock the next morning they presented themselves at the Albion Hotel, Manchester, in a Wilmslow post chaise, ready to commence their nefarious operation.

At eight o'clock on Tuesday morning a carriage was driven to the Liverpool premises of Mrs Daulby. Edward's manservant alighted from it and presented a letter to Mrs Daulby, claiming he had brought it with him from Shrigley Hall. The precise contents of the letter were as follows:

Shrigley,
Monday night, half-past twelve
Madam

I write to you by the desire of Mrs Turner of Shrigley, who has been seized with a sudden and dangerous attack of paralysis. Mr Turner is unfortunately from home but has been sent for and Mrs Turner wishes to see her daughter immediately. A steady servant will take this letter and my carriage to you to fetch Miss Turner, and I beg that no time may be lost in her departure, as, though I do not think Mrs Turner in immediate danger, it is possible she may soon became incapable of recognising anyone.

Mrs Turner particularly wishes that her daughter may not be informed of the extent of her danger as, without this precaution Miss Turner might be very anxious on the journey; and this house is so crowded, and in such confusion and alarm, that Mrs Turner does not wish anyone to accompany her daughter. The servant is instructed not to let the boys drive too fast, as Miss T. is rather fearful in a carriage.

   I am, madam your obedient servant
   John Ainsworth, MD

   The best thing to say to Miss T, is that Mrs T. wishes to have her daughter home rather sooner, for the approaching removal to the new house, and the servant is instructed to give no other reason in case Miss Turner should ask any questions. Mrs Turner is very anxious that her daughter should not be frightened and trusts to your judgement to prevent it. She also desires me to add that her sister, or niece, or myself should they continue unable, will not fail to write to you by post.

As can be seen, the letter had a strong authentic ring about it and Miss Turner was immediately informed that her presence was required at home. The only query that arose in young Ellen's mind was that the servant sent to collect her was a total stranger. The servant, Thevenot by name, rose glibly to the challenge and explained that in consequence of Mr Turner having taken a new mansion, he had made some alteration in his establishment and engaged him as a butler, to replace the person who had filled the position previously. He added that the carriage would return by way of Manchester for him to fulfil another duty before proceeding to Shrigley. Suspicion was allayed, Miss Turner took her seat, and the coach set off on its journey.

Upon reaching Manchester the coach stopped at the door of the Albion Hotel and the young lady was invited within and shown into a private room. Shortly afterwards Edward Wakefield joined her and instantly caused her some unease, being a stranger to her, but on being told he had come to her from her papa, she remained. Introducing himself, Wakefield adopted an ingratiating persona and confessed that she had been the victim of a clever and justified ruse to remove her from her school in order to hide the real reason from her teacher and fellow pupils. The true reason, he said, was the sudden, serious state of her father's business affairs. He then introduced his brother William to her, telling her that they were directed to escort her to her father as quickly as possible. They ordered post-horses to be instantly got ready and were soon on their way.

Her destination, Wakefield told her, was Kendal, where her father awaited her, but at the end of this long journey, predictably, disappointment awaited the poor girl and her abductor found it necessary to feed her further untruths to ease her anxious state. Her father's dilemma, he explained, had been caused by the failure of Messrs Daintry and Ryle's bank at Macclesfield. Wakefield's uncle, a Kendal banker, he went on, had loaned her father a great sum of money to cushion the damage but the failure of the bank at Blackburn had added further grief to her father's position. However, her papa's legal adviser, Mr Grimsditch, had formulated a plan, whereby manipulating certain assets and transferring property to Ellen, the estate would belong to her husband, should she acquire one quickly! He, Wakefield, had been asked to fill this role - with considerable initial embarrassment, he felt bound to admit - but had finally agreed and now Miss Turner had the choice of accompanying him to Gretna Green for marriage or have her father turned out of his home and answer to sheriff's officers!

Love for her father won the day and Ellen agreed to extend her journey to Carlisle and thence to Gretna, and in due course the marriage ceremony was performed by the blacksmith in the customary manner; no residence qualification was required in those days.

On returning to Carlisle, Ellen was informed that her father, having received confirmation of the marriage - and his own salvation - had returned to Shrigley Hall, whither they were to follow him, but having reached Leeds, Edward 'recollected' that he had an appointment in Paris which he had to keep in the ensuing week. He and his bride would not, therefore, have time to call at Shrigley, but he pretended to send William there to report to her parents on their daughter's happiness and well-being. William, he claimed, would rejoin them in London later.

Edward and Ellen arrived at Blake's Hotel, Hanover Square, at 11.30 on the night of Friday,19th March, to be told by a messenger that Mr Turner and William Wakefield had already left for France, a further lie readily accepted by Ellen. A chaise was ordered to take the couple to Dover and from there they would take the first packet to Calais.

At this point only the conspirators knew of the abduction, and how Ellen's parents first became aware of this major crisis in their lives is not certain. It is known that Edward Wakefield penned a letter to Mr Turner at Carlisle, upon leaving Scotland, notifying him of the marriage, but may have arranged for posting to be delayed in order to give the couple time to cross the Channel. It is known also that, brief as their stay in London had been, Edward had arranged for the marriage to be formally announced in The Times, making an open claim, it would seem, that his union with Ellen was a normal, loving contract.

One way or another then, in those pre-railway/electric telegraph days, the dreadful news reached the Turner family, with what affect it is difficult to imagine. Their initial shock and horror was further compounded when Mrs Daulby, Ellen's teacher, revealed the full seriousness of the offence on production of the highly incriminating letter.

Mr Turner hastened to London for the purpose of procuring such aid as could be afforded by the police of the metropolis. On learning that his daughter had been taken to the Continent he sent a party of four in pursuit: his brother, Mr Grimsditch, his solicitor; Mr Critchley, a Macclesfield silk manufacturer and banker, and a Bow Street officer.

In the meantime, a letter was received by Mrs Turner from Edward Wakefield, dated Calais, in which the writer repeated the declaration that he had married her daughter and admitted that his own persuasive influence had been the key factor. He added: *"Miss Turner is fondly attached to me, and I do assure you, my dear madam, that it shall be the anxious endeavour of my life to promote her happiness by every means in my power."*

Upon the landing of the pursuing quartet at Calais, the first persons they saw were the young lady they sought and Edward Wakefield, who were walking on the pier. Ellen rushed to her uncle and expressed deep relief that he had come to take her home, whereupon Wakefield objected strongly and forthwith appealed to the civil authorities of the town to support a husband's claim to keep his wife with him. Questioned by the mayor, Ellen denounced Edward as a fraudster and artful abductor. Edward Wakefield, finding his plans completely frustrated, said to the uncle, *"Then, sir, you may dispose of your niece as you think proper but you receive her at my hands as a pure and spotless virgin."* He made a similar statement in writing. Mr Turner, his niece and party, were then free to return to England and a subdued Edward Gibbon Wakefield completed his journey to Paris alone.

As details of the abduction spread throughout Britain there was widespread anger against Edward Wakefield and his cohorts and an eagerness for their arrest and speedy punishment. Warrants were issued against the Wakefield brothers for abduction and William Wakefield was apprehended within days. Edward Wakefield returned to England to share the fate of his accomplices. A further indictment was preferred against the brothers, their stepmother and Edward's servant for conspiracy. True bills were returned against the brothers and stepmother and reduced to misdemeanour in respect of the servant, who was in France anyway.

The legal process was bedevilled with confusion and uncertainty, argument and counter-argument, and it was not until Friday, 23rd March, 1827 - a year and 16 days after Miss Turner's abduction - that the trio, each pleading not guilty, was brought before the court at Lancaster. There was nationwide interest in the proceedings and great excitement in the town itself. All three were found guilty, to await sentence.

Seven weeks later the brothers were brought before the King's Bench at Westminster. Edward G. Wakefield was sentenced to three years imprisonment at Newgate, his brother William for a similar term at Lancaster Castle. Mrs Frances Wakefield was not brought up for judgement, the generous feelings of Mr Turner, much injured as his family had been, preventing him proceeding with harshness against her.

The question of the legality of the marriage was involved in so much doubt that it was finally annulled by special Act of Parliament. In 1828 Ellen Turner married Thomas Legh of Lyme, but there was to be no happy ending for this tragic girl. She died in childbirth in 1831, just 19 years old. The child, Ellen Jane survived, and in the fullness of time inherited Shrigley Hall.

Edward Wakefield's stay in Newgate Prison proved to be a major turning point in his life. Contemplating emigration once he had served his sentence, he began a careful study of colonial affairs, and particularly the subject of colonisation. He was surprised by the absence of any attempt to direct colonial enterprise on scientific principles. In his *Letter From Sydney* written in prison he originated the plan of subsidised emigration from Britain and proposed the sale of small units of crown land in the colonies, to subsidise colonisation by the poor, rather than by convicts.

His proposals, which came to be known as Wakefield Settlements, were adopted in 1831, and in the South Australian Act of 1834. He influenced the South Australian Association (1836), formed the New Zealand Association (1837) and inspired the Durham Report (1839) on colonial affairs in Canada, which he visited in 1838, 1841, and 1843.

The importance of Wakefield's achievements in colonial matters cannot be overestimated. He brought to the subject for the first time the mind of the philosopher and statesman. The great flaw in his character was lack of scruple in selecting the means for attaining his ends, but to him is largely due the systematised and aided emigration that founded modern Canada, Australia and New Zealand.

In 1846 he succumbed to overwork and became seriously ill. Somewhat recovered he left England for Wellington, New Zealand in 1853, but his renewed enthusiasm for his work was short-lived and his health completely broke down a year later. He died in New Zealand, where he is revered to this day, on 16th May, 1862. His son Edward Jerningham Wakefield survived him. His daughter, Susan Priscilla did not.

31

Roe Record Excitement

Good friends, bless 'em, continue to loan me items of interest from Macclesfield's past. A recent package, handed to me quite unceremoniously in a plastic shopping bag, contained a few old newspapers (upon which I may choose to comment at some future date) and several folded documents.

These proved to be properly drawn-up legal agreements in copper-plate writing. Some were apprenticeship indentures which, although interesting, did not excite my pulse in the manner achieved by two others in particular.

These latter were linked documents, identically prepared, and constituted an agreement between two gentlemen of Macclesfield. No great issue was involved and it is perhaps best that the wording of the first paragraph of text is reproduced in order to convey flavour and information to the reader:

First it is severally agreed by the said parties for their mutual convenience to make an Exchange of Ground and a general alteration in the wall fence or boundary which separates the garden of the said Thomas Sheldon lying and being on the west side of the house in which he now lives in a certain street in Macclesfield aforesaid called the Barn Street and now in his possession together with another garden of the said Thomas Sheldon lying antiguous to the south end of the said first mentioned garden and now in the possession of Joseph Stokes from the garden of the said Charles Roe lately made and enclosed out of a certain field called the Barn field and from the road leading to the said Charles Roe's garden.

There is much more to follow dealing with an assortment of precise measurements and all of it couched in like fashion. The two documents were signed, one by the illustrious Mr Roe of Macclesfield history - the cause of my excitement - the other by Mr Sheldon, just before Christmas, 1755, and both were officially stamped and sealed. This date, incidentally, was a mere ten years after the Young Pretender and his kilted army tarried briefly in our town as they approached the end of their forlorn trek south. I cannot resist the temptation of placing the antiquity of these documents into fuller perspective by pointing out that George II was the reigning monarch, that in the same year James Cook enlisted in the Royal Navy and that 14 more years would pass before New Zealand and Australia would be discovered by this intrepid explorer.

Further, that as Messrs Roe and Sheldon signed each other's document with their sepia-inked quills, Horatio Nelson and Arthur Wellesley, 1st Duke of Wellington, had yet to be born; as had, during the remainder of that century, artists Constable and Turner and literary giants Scott, Southey, Austen, Shelley and Keats. Nearer to home, when the Duke of Bridgewater asked James Brindley, the great engineer (who had served his apprenticeship at Gurnett Smithy) to build him the canal that was to be the first of a network soon to cover the countryside, these two documents had been slumbering in

The former Macclesfield windmill (Windmill Street) after it had been moved to Kerridge.

Broken Cross in the 1920s

their pigeon-hole for close on 15 years.

Macclesfield was made a Chartered Borough in 1262 and it is thanks to Charles Roe that the 1755 date on the documents is, arguably, the next most important date in the town's annals, for it was in that year, Roe, hitherto engaged in the manufacture of buttons and silk twist, became so impressed with the success of silk throwing, first at Derby then at Congleton, that he decided that he would commence such business in Macclesfield.

During the next year he built what became known as Depot Mill on Park Green, or Parsonage Green as it was known at that time. This decision by Charles Roe soon resulted in the town becoming the chief centre in England for this branch of the silk industry.

Only three years later this remarkable man's interest in mineralogy resulted in the establishment of extensive copper works on Macclesfield Common and a large windmill was built to grind the ore. In a later era this windmill was moved and re-built at Kerridge and many of today's folk will remember it as I do.

These documents, therefore, which it has been such a joy for me to hold and behold, pre-date this built-up common area of the town which contains such streets as Windmill, Calamine (a zinc-based ore used in the smelting and manufacturing process), Brasshouse and Copper.

The photographer here was within a few yards of where Geoffrey was employed by

St Paul's Church - looking over from Sparrow Park at the rebuilding of Central Station

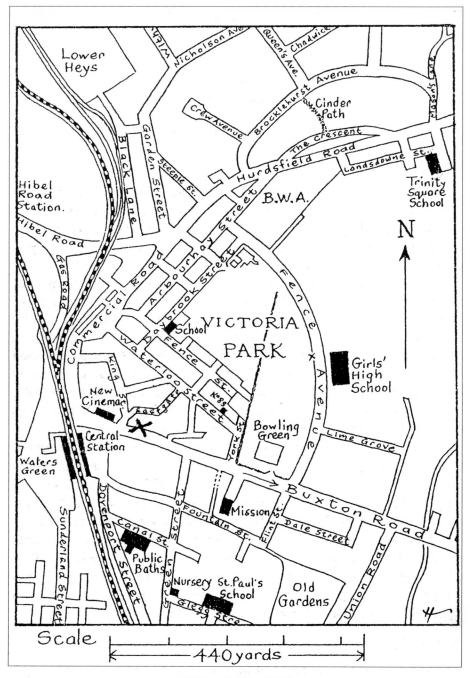

LOWER HURDSFIELD
The home of Frank Burgess is marked with a cross, just to the right of the New Cinema.

32
My Early Years
by Frank Burgess edited by Geoff

Introducing Frank Burgess

When *Old Macc* magazine was launched by Doug and Hilary Pickford late in 1996 and I accepted a limited role at the Macclesfield end of the business, my recreational strolling, hitherto somewhat haphazard, took on a more positive aspect. I received invitations to other people's homes to peruse photographs, old documents and maps and to listen to family stories of the past.

One of these kind persons was Mrs Margaret Burgess who telephoned me towards the end of 1997, less than a year after suffering the loss of her husband, Frank. Margaret, as I am now privileged to call her, initially concealed the light under her own bushel, so eager was she to interest me in an assortment of little notebooks containing Frank's jottings, accumulated over the years. I accepted a loan of the notebooks to study at my leisure in my own home, and then asked questions about Margaret herself, and to my delight discovered her bushel-light shone brilliantly! Old Macc has benefited from time to time with articles from this gifted lady.

My assessment of Frank's writings over those next few weeks proved to be an absorbing and joyous exercise. Confining my interest from Frank's birth in 1915 to the end of his teenage years in 1935, the stories I selected for publication lent themselves easily to chronological sequence and divided readily into eight serialized parts for publication during 1998 and 1999.

In this book, again with Margaret's permission, I have achieved another ambition, I have made space available for Frank's story to be told, in full, in one volume, because I believe it deserves to be. My only literary contribution is the story's simple title and the brief headings. I'm delighted to have Frank on board. Thank you, Margaret!

Part 1: First Impressions

One of my earliest recollections of those post first world war days is of the new parson we had at our church, or rather Chapel as it was then called by all good Methodists. It was on Park Green and Mr John Gibbon had just returned from the forces as a chaplain, and I can see him now at that first service in his army uniform. I can almost hear him, too, because he was so forceful a speaker and followed the traditions of all good Welsh preachers by shouting and hitting the pulpit desk with his fists.

I was not a little frightened by this extraordinary figure in uniform waving his arms about. Actually, he was only of small stature and after his first service, having donned the normal black suit, he held no more terrors for me although his antics in the pulpit in no way abated. Out of the pulpit (or should I say offstage?) he was a most charming man and I got to know the family very well, for they were with us for 10 years, which for a Methodist Chapel was most unusual.

The manse was a little further up Buxton Road from our house and I very often went up in those between-years to play with his only son, Gaunt. Gaunt had a bigger Hornby train set than I had, but he always envied my Royal Scot class locomotive - the massive looking 4-6-0 plus tender - which was my pride and joy.

The main reason why he enjoyed coming down to our house was that we had in common a love of tin soldiers. They were made of lead, actually, and were far superior to the present-day models both in attractiveness and correctness of their markings. First we used to form them into impressive ranks with an officer at the head of each rank, sword in hand. For the first rank I always insisted on Grenadiers, then the Coldstreams... then the Scots Guards bringing up the rear because part of this battalion, of course, was made up of pipers in their kilts. Behind these came the cavalry, with another resplendent officer in scarlet, blue and gold, to lead them. When we tired of warfare we turned our attention to civil engineering in the form of Meccano.

Gaunt also envied me this because I was adding to it every week. All my pocket money went on more gear wheels, eccentric wheels, rubber tyres for making motor cars, shafting and pulling wheels for intricate machinery, so we could ignore the manual and build anything we liked. After a while we owned a clockwork motor, which added realism. We were then able to construct a steam engine - run by clockwork!

Gaunt's father wasn't approved of by a large section of his congregation. It was whispered that he liked a drop of the rather potent golden-coloured liquid which wasn't mentioned in the best Methodist circles;

and to add to this he wrote plays! Whoever heard of a play writing, whisky-drinking Methodist parson who kept shocking hours? For it was said that small groups of men emerged from the manse at all times of the night and early morning! But people had to speak as they found because he did a tremendous lot of work in the circuit, visiting hospitals and poor homes, rarely with empty hands.

The turning point came with the performance of his first play called *The Miner's Mark* which he produced himself in the schoolroom and also took the leading role. The action took place in a Welsh coal mine and I still remember the shattering effect on the audience when disaster struck - when the 'prop' pit props gave way and the 'mine' caved in. The noise and the lighting effects were brilliantly handled and not one of us dared breathe until the dust had settled and we could see the results of such dramatic force.

From then on Mr Gibbon was regarded as a genius! People began to make excuses to each other for his "funny little ways" and as my mother was in business, I used to overhear some of her customers' conversations when they visited the shop.

"Well of course", said one well-respected lady, *"most clever people are a little eccentric, aren't they?"* to much nodding of heads.

"But then," said another, *"not like us you know"*....and so on.

So ends the saga of one Mr Gibbon, who I am sure looked upon himself as one of the humblest of men. But he had made his mark far more effectively through his play than through all the shouting and gesticulating from the pulpit. All was forgiven, even to the odd sight to any caller at his front door of the rather grim-looking flintlock pistol hanging in the hall!

When I was seven or so I went to my first funeral. A Mrs Andrews, a very good friend of my Granny's (my mother's mother who lived with us) had been scratched by her pet black cat and had died from blood poisoning. Why I went I had no idea but my Grannie and I travelled some 25 miles by train to a place called Dewsbury and there I dutifully viewed my first body. I don't remember any kind of emotion as I gazed at a face I'd never seen before, but it wasn't pleasant. When the funeral party departed I was left in the house with a neighbour, just a shadowy figure. I was on the lookout all the time for the guilty cat which had killed my Granny's friend. It didn't show up so I concluded it must have gone off with a witch.

Coming round, as it were, after my bout of thoughtfulness, I intended to

have a good look at my companion's face, only to find that she had
disappeared and I was alone in that very unpleasant room. Had she had a
hooked nose I wondered? And I was no further forward when the funeral
party came back for tea in the next room because everybody was dressed in
deep black, and there were noses of all shapes and sizes!

Part 2: School and other lessons

My schooldays were very leisurely affairs all through. In the first class at St.
Paul's I played with a lot of sand and plasticine, watched over by a kindly old
lady named Miss Fearn and every now and again, Miss Walker, the head
teacher of the junior school would stroll into the classroom and exude benign
charm. There never seemed to be any noise - we youngsters were always
engrossed in what we were doing. Boredom was not a part of the school's
curriculum in those days.

I looked forward to reading lessons because there were always books
around the house at home. My first experience at putting letters together to
form words came from sitting in front of the fire in the living room and
gazing at a black-leaded nameplate screwed on to the top of the firegrate.
The inscription read: CHAS. A. DAY. MACCLESFIELD. Now this puzzled
me for a long time. When I was able to put the last word together, MACC-
LES-FIELD, and was told it was the name of the town we lived in, the
sentence (as I thought) was even more intriguing.... If it meant 'C HAS A
DAY' why had they left out the little word 'IN' to read 'C HAS A DAY IN
MACCLESFIELD'? And who was 'C'? The initial of my father's Christian
name? Or my mother's? Or Granny's?

Not knowing their names, of course (children never did in those days),
I couldn't tell. So in the end - having noticed the full stops - I was forced to
ask Granny and the mystery was solved. How silly, I thought, that CHAS.
could possibly stand for Charles. Household fittings didn't cater for child
readers!

I was getting on very well with my books when I had the misfortune of
being laid low with rheumatic fever at the age of eight and I was off school
(so they told me) for six months. I had just begun to have piano lessons, too,
which I also missed through being in bed. Not that I ever enjoyed scales
very much but even 'The Bluebells of Scotland' seemed more attractive when
one couldn't get to the piano.

During this time my musical activities weren't entirely starved, because after a little performance on a small mouth organ I was presented with a large shiny new one. This was followed by a melodeon, the fore-runner of the piano accordion, and then to my great delight my father bought me a half-size violin which I strove to get a tune out of.

By this time I was ready to go back to school and on my first week back I had the most memorable experience of my childhood. The top forms always got together on Friday afternoons for music and they must have put in a lot of practise while I had been away. I've forgotten which lesson our class was doing, when all at once the choir began to

An early studio portrait of Frank.

sing 'Land of Hope and Glory'. Our classroom was near to the hall and the effect on me was shattering.

Never in my life had I heard music like this before and I can remember standing up and beating time with my fist on the desk in front of me - oblivious of all else. Even when Mr Armitt stood in front of me I took no notice, and it was only when he slapped my face did I realise that I should have been working quietly at my lessons; but I'd had my first taste of uplifting music and for those moments of sheer joy I shall ever be thankful.

As it turned out Elgar must have been the first composer I made contact with because a little later on my piano teacher, a Mr Wilfred Southwell from Todmorden, gave me a gramophone record of 'Salut d'amour'. It hadn't the power of the Pomp and Circumstance march, it is true, but quite a catchy tune for a youngster.

That reminds me. Mr Southwell was my second piano teacher. My first was a lady named Miss Wain who had a room above Harrop's Music Shop in Chestergate. I didn't like Miss Wain at all. She couldn't have been a day over 35 but that was a great age to me. She was not a pleasant person and kept a twelve inch ruler handy to rap your knuckles if you made a mistake - and I made plenty. I must have done because I remember my mother going up to see her to ask how anyone could be expected to play properly with sore fingers! Needless to say I then went to Mr Southwell. He was a very merry little man, about the same age as Miss Wain actually, but behind his spectacles there was always a twinkle.

When I got to know the face of Schubert, that was Mr Southwell! He didn't mind mistakes at all. He said it would all come out right in the end and that Beethoven didn't mind mistakes anyway. That set me thinking. I'd heard the 'Moonlight Sonata' on records and I asked whether I could study it.

"The 'Moonlight'?" he laughed. There was a little silence. I wondered for a moment whether he knew it! I asked him. *"Oh yes,"* he replied and began to rattle off that tempestuous finale. *"I'm afraid you won't be ready for that for some time, my boy."*

"But-but-but", I stammered, feeling very guilty. *"I thought perhaps the* **first** *movement."*

"Oh that", he smiled. *"We'll see - in a little while. We must put in a lot more practise with our E major and C sharp minor scales, mustn't we?"* I humbly agreed.

I must add here that for a slightly higher fee Mr Southwell came to give me piano lessons at home, which suited him fine, because to eke out a meagre existence he'd taken on the job as organist at the local Spiritualist Church.

He confided to my family that if his parents got to know they would immediately recall him back to the bosom of the Church of England in Todmorden! And that would make things very awkward for him because he had just become engaged to an oatcake baker's daughter in Macclesfield named Elsie Ratcliffe.

He enjoyed telling us of little incidents which occurred during what he called the 'seances' at his adopted church. They amused him very much. My mother told him that she had been to one of the services at the church out of curiosity and had sat on the end of a form. When the congregation had risen unexpectedly the form tipped and deposited my mother on the floor. At this

Mr Southwell collapsed with such mirth that his spectacles fell off and tears ran down his face. He was a kind, simple, uncomplicated soul, who enjoyed simple uncomplicated things like sitting at the piano and playing a good hymn tune.

I forgot to mention earlier that after Mr Armitt (nicknamed 'Cherry') had brought me to my senses with the slap on the face following my Elgar experience, he came back to me not a half hour later and in some confusion apologised for this rash act of his. He spoke very quietly, with a very red face, and told me that my mother had just been to school to tell him about a medical specialist's report on my heart condition following my bout of rheumatic fever, and that I was not to go outside during lesson breaks to play games, etc.

So after this incident I sat and read a book and Mr Armitt and I were the best of friends!

Part 3: Family, Trade and Property

My Great Grandpa and my Grandpa were family butchers by trade and my father being the eldest son he carried on the business.

All three were named George. The first George had two sons, George and Peter, who were both butchers. Peter had his business premises on Hurdsfield Road while Grandpa's was on Buxton Road. Peter lived at Shakespeare House which divides the two Buxton roads at the junction of the old and the new. Peter and Elizabeth had one son (father's cousin) named Richard who became an auctioneer with Stanley Turner and later owned his own business in Whitchurch, Salop. 'Sammy Dick', as father always called him, was the only member of the family to distinguish himself in the Great War, having become a Captain in the Cavalry.

My Grandpa married into a tailoring family consisting of the Dexters and the Eatons, both families with shops in Mill Street. 'Dolly' Dexter was my Grandmother and a grander grandmother no-one could wish to have. She must have been very pretty in her young days for it was said that all the young bucks of that period were after her hand and the charm that went with it. Grandpa was very handsome too - for it was he who won Grandma (I was allowed to call her that - she never could be Grannie like Mum's mum) who was very aloof. Even up to the time of her death at the age of 85 she walked upright and with marvellous grace, being very slim, her hands clasped in front of her and wearing always a white lace cap on her snow white hair.

I said she was aloof. Yes, almost to the point of being autocratic - in fact I was completely beneath her notice. I never got near enough to hold a conversation with her; the charming smile had to be my portion. She had no time for small boys, and even less for my mother! She considered that her eldest son had married beneath him and that was that.

My mother was always referred to as 'Mrs George', whereas all my father's brothers (but one) had married a 'Mary' so they became Fred's Mary, Harry's Mary and Arthur's Mary, although in this last, Grandma met her match. She alone refused to pay homage so she was crossed off the visiting list.

There were two more sons, Jack who married Emma and Frank the youngest (whose namesake I was). He was killed in the war in 1916, aged 26. Aunt Jane, Aunt Elizabeth, Aunt Louie and Aunt Harriet presented a formidable quartet to me at first but as I got to know them they were all very charming and had Grandpa's sense of humour, without losing Grandma's polish. All the girls and my father were educated at a private school, but as the other boys came along they were sent to St. Paul's.

My aunts all played the piano and my father had a good ear for music which the rest of the family did not. I really enjoyed going to hear Aunt Harriet's gramophone (with a horn) because she had records of Handel's Messiah, a work I couldn't hear enough of - so much so that my dear Aunt bought me an alabaster bust of Handel which is still one of my prized possessions.

Aunt Harriet liked to play Schubert at her piano in Buxton Road. Aunt Elizabeth played Chopin at her house, 142 Great King Street. Aunt Jane had married a violinist and my parents and I were treated to small recitals whenever we visited them at their house in Gurnett, on the way to Langley. Aunt Louie was married to an oboist so we had duets there too at their home in Hurdsfield Road, just below the canal bridge on the right - a nice old world cottage set well back from the road.

The three properties in Buxton Road owned by Grandpa consisted of the butcher's shop with the large family house behind it, number 37. Then came number 39 which was occupied by an old lady named Mrs Cooper whose husband was the Waterman on the Corporation and a member of the fire brigade. It was always exciting, whenever there was a fire somewhere, to see him dashing down the road to the fire station, putting his coat and helmet on as he ran.

He was in the habit of visiting the Dog and Partridge every evening - the pub was a little further up the road on the other side - to which no objection was raised by my non-drinking family, but a strict rule was enforced that as soon as the pub closed at 10-30 p.m. he would come to his back door by way of the entry next to our house, bolt the entry door and shout as he passed our window, *"fastened up",* when we would call back, *"good night."* This was one way of getting him to keep decent hours!

Between his house and the entry was number 41 where we lived and mother had her greengrocer's shop. Behind these three houses was a long yard and an even longer row of old cottages which by my young days were used as stables, cowshed, sheep pen, pig sty and slaughter house, and one used by my mother as a fruit and vegetable warehouse.

Mr Cooper, almost at retiring age, had a bad accident to do with road works and pipe-laying, and died shortly afterwards in the Infirmary. Mrs Cooper's four sons Bob, Syd, George and Jack, and her daughter Evelyn, were all now married, and she was now living alone. It was someone's bright idea to put our Broadwood piano in her house and reduce her rent from five shillings weekly to 3s/6d. For one thing it would be company for her if I did my practising there and for another it would he quieter for me to get down to my studying.

Probably the real reason was that I was cluttering the place up a bit as well as distracting the customers in the shop. The arrangement worked very well and I was able to play for hours at a time without being disturbed - Mrs Cooper nearly always being asleep in her rocking chair. One of my favourite pieces was the slow movement from one of Beethoven's Sonatas, and I once asked Mrs Cooper if she liked it. *"Well,"* came the shattering reply, *"I might like it better if I knew the words!"*

I got my first experience of accompaniment at that house because Bob Cooper's daughter Annie was going 'steady' with a boy called Harold Galley and besides being a fair performer on the violin (taught by his father) he also had a good baritone voice. So, much to the annoyance of Annie (I learned later) we spent a number of evenings a week, he either fiddling or singing and I accompanying him.

Every Saturday evening the Cooper family had a get-together and played cards and later repaired to the Dog and Partridge. This was the signal on those particular evenings for me to go home, to collect a small basin and go across the road to the fish and chip shop owned by a Mr and Mrs Waterhouse - Mr Waterhouse was the postman in our district. What I collected in my basin wasn't either fish or chips but small butter beans to which I was addicted, and you could get the basin half-full for one penny - with vinegar!

It was at one of those convivial gatherings at the Cooper establishment that I played my first hand at whist. I did it with much trepidation and guilt because I knew my father would be very angry if he found out. It was only after a solemn promise from Mrs Cooper that it was not to be broadcast that I consented (having been invited to play so many times that it got very embarrassing to refuse any more - but I never took part in gambling!)

Part 4: First Love... and the School Board

I began to spend more time at home in the evenings in 1927 after we got our first real wireless set. I say real because the first one we had was a crystal set where you had to play with a thing called a 'cat's whisker' (a very fine wire) to make it connect and get a tune or whatever else there was going on at the time. Coupled with this intriguing ritual, one had to wear headphones so it wasn't much pleasure really.

But the real set was a different matter. It had a loudspeaker, rather like a gramophone horn except it was curved with a bell-shaped end. The set was built for us by Mrs Cooper's son in law Joe Goodwin, who in after years was to become my radio mechanic.

Looking through the *Radio Times* one week I was fascinated by an account of the following evening's Promenade Concerts given over to one particular composer per evening. There was no-one more surprised than my parents when I asked to tune in to these programmes. Mother thought it was only an excuse to prolong my bed time, but my father, bless him (although he wasn't really interested) said, *"Give the boy a chance. If he enjoys them, let him listen."* So that was a great milestone in my early childhood; well, I would be perhaps 12 at the time.

I must admit that I found Bach rather heavy going at first. He hadn't the instant appeal for me that Handel had, for instance, but I was converted by a beautiful contralto voice singing in one of the cantatas. Her name was Betty Bannerman, and a few weeks later the *Radio Times* published a picture of her. That did it! She was the first woman I ever fell in love with. Her voice had come first, but this photograph, taken head and shoulders in profile, looking upwards, really captured me, heart and soul. At the end of the week I cut out the photograph and fitted it into a small gilt frame and put it by my bed, without a word to anyone. And no one ever said a word about it either.

Her age at that time must have been somewhere between 25 and 30. I believe that when she retired from singing, she came to live in a large house in Cheshire between Siddington and Somerford.

Getting back to St Paul's School, my main interest was reading books and writing and I always came out on top with composition, dictation and spelling. I was never very interested in arithmetic. The nearest I ever got to boredom was playing about with figures. Numbers to me were dead things jumbled together. Not with words... Ah, that was very different. The construction of sentences had endless possibilities. They set the imagination alight, whatever the subject one was writing about and my main interest was history and still is, apart from music of course.

Mr Wood, the master of form three, found a very handy weapon for non-attenders to his discourses, in the form of a large T-square with which he leaned over from his position in front of class to tap any head as far back as the back row! There were four heads for some reason that were never tapped in this way because the owners were sitting at four desks put together down the side of the classroom: Frank Turner, Frank Barlow, Frank Burgess and John Taylor, I think, were supposed to be some sort of example to the rest of the class.

Mr Shaw, the Head, used to drop in at odd times during class and tell short anecdotes to brighten us up - or so it seemed. I can only remember one of these which concerned a large poster stuck onto a wall bearing the words, "WANTED - BILL STICKERS". The poster's seemingly innocent legend, the headmaster explained, caused much consternation to a certain individual who read it -- namely, Bill Stickers himself!

I had another long spell off school and had to visit a heart specialist called Sir William Milligan in John Street, Manchester, at frequent intervals; Dr Proudfoot being on hand almost constantly. When in better health I used to take orders out for Father in the Buxton Road area, which covered as far afield as Eddisbury Hall, owned then by a Manchester cotton manufacturer. A telephone was installed in the shop, more or less for this personage's benefit - but Father was sometimes a little annoyed when they rang up for two lamb chops to be delivered ...

Apart from his Maxwell car, Father bought a new Morris van and had his name painted on the sides. This was to deliver orders to Broken Cross, Gawsworth, Langley, etc., and to outlying farms. A large refrigerator was also fitted in one of the out-buildings which would hold several sheep, pigs and 'quarters' of beef.

Health Officer Joseph Hermann used to pay regular calls and so did the Vet, as other butchers had the facilities of our slaughterhouse, like Billy Kirk, Bill Slack, Dobson & Thornhill, etc.

There was a constant stream of livestock about our Buxton Road premises. I remember on one particular occasion a cow missed its aim going through the entry door, it burst open Mother's greengrocer's shop door, ran through the shop to the accompanying screams of Mother and Grannie, and got stuck in the passage leading to the living room. Someone had to go through the back door and guide it backwards by its horns! Dad I think.

A rather odd little figure of a man used to be constantly on our doorstep during my school-age years. He always dressed in a dark grey suit and wore a bowler hat, and was what we now call the School Attendance Officer, but in those days was known as the 'School Board'. So if anyone ever played truant, it was said, "The School Board will be after you!" His name was Mr Allen and he lived just round the corner in Green Street. As I was very rarely at school, through some illness or other, he was a very persistent visitor, although he very well knew the circumstances.

He would come into the shop with the same old gambit: *"Mrs Burgess, your son is away from school again, and....."* To which my mother's reply was, *"I know Mr Allen... he's here beside me."* *"When will he be ready to come back?"* *"I've no idea".* *"But you must have some idea."* (rather sharply). *"When the doctor says so, he will come back. Now, Mr Allen, if you don't mind...."*

"But I have my duty to do." On one such occasion my Grannie appeared at this juncture and said: *"Then go and do it somewhere else - we've no time to be bothered."*

These rather unpleasant visits went on until I believe my father wrote to the Education Office very strongly and told Mother that if the man called again she must send for him (my father) right away. The day came, and my father appeared and spoke very quietly. *"Mr Allen, I have written to the*

Lower Hurdsfield, Fence Street with Daybrook School at end.

Lower Hurdsfield - Commercial Road area showing opening to Fence Street.
These photographs, and those that follow, are of the area Frank new and loved.
Behind his home on Buxton Road, the area remained virtually unchanged from the
time of Frank's birth until the widespread demolition of the 1960s.

Education Authorities to tell them to keep you away from these premises. Did you know?"

    "Yes, but my duty...."

    "Then will you go quietly, or shall I send for the police?"

Needless to say, we never saw Mr Allen again.

Part 5: Florence and a Funeral

At about the age of twelve I persuaded Mother to buy me a full-sized violin and had great fun with it until I decided it was time to do some serious study. So I approached the younger son of a family we'd always known, who lived on Buxton Road, and asked him if he would teach me to play.

    Willie Mottershead and his sister Doreen did a lot of playing together, Doreen being a good pianist. It was decided that he should take me on for a few weeks, without fee, to see how I shaped. After that, having satisfied my teacher I was in earnest, we began serious study and I reached the standard where we could play duets, and even trios with Doreen at the piano. It was great fun and I spent hours at home practising in my bedroom.

    As I have mentioned before the house between the two shops on Buxton Road also belonged to the family and was occupied by Mrs Cooper. I already had my piano in her downstairs room and it was decided that as she lived alone she could manage without her front bedroom! So with another reduction in her rent front 3/6 per week to 2 shillings, Father called in his brother Fred, the builder, to knock a hole through from our front bedroom to hers and make a doorway, sealing up the intervening one which led to the old lady's back bedroom.

    It was a good large front room and I insisted on decorating it myself, as it was meant for me. I managed to dissuade Mother from buying *"just the wallpaper for that room"* - a pattern of very large flowers - and buying instead a very plain creamy paper. *"Why, goodness knows?"* she said, but I think when I'd finished it she had to admit that at least it looked smart.

    By the time I'd put up black and white etchings in black frames (instead of the usual Landseer type paintings of animals in gold frames), and got my sizeable collection of books housed in bookcases, it was more like a study than a bedroom. Again I have my father to thank for his tolerance.

    So poor old Mrs Cooper was beset behind and before. If I wasn't playing the piano in her living room, 1 was playing the violin in her bedroom!

Asked whether she was being disturbed at all, she put on an agonised smile and said, *"Oh no, it's company!"*

I was just approaching school-leaving age when Grandpa was taken ill with pleurisy, which turned to pneumonia. They had a full time maid (I mean the 'live-in' kind) who just at this crucial time decided to leave and another younger girl was taken on, whose home was in Congleton. Well, it seems that during Grandpa's illness, whilst the family was sat upstairs with him, poor young Florence (I think that was her name) got lonely sitting by herself at the fire. I don't know whose brilliant idea it was, but I was asked to go and keep her company.

At first it was a bit awkward, for we had little to talk about, but as she was about 18 months older than I was, she sort of took over, and suggested that we sat at the table (on the couch) and played games. We used to get quite excited about snakes and ladders, Ludo, and most of all, draughts. They were interesting enough to start with, but I began to get bored and wished Grandpa would get well - or something (he was 86) - so that I could get back to playing the piano.

I must have spoken my thoughts aloud one evening because Florence produced a set of tiddly winks for a change, and when Aunt Harriet came downstairs, which was the sign that I could go home, Florence came to the back door with me and kissed me on the cheek, and said *"Goodnight"*

The following evening Florence came to the door with me again to say goodnight and this time she held her cheek to be kissed. Should I? Did one do this sort of thing? I hesitated, then as the voice of my aunt was heard calling *"Florence"*, I pecked her on the cheek and hurried home. Yes, I thought, tiddly winks certainly was an improvement on the other games.

The following evening, though, was to be the final round, and the last time I saw Florence. Halfway through our game she took my hand and held it. I looked at her and she looked at me, smiling. Then she put her face close to mine and just rubbed noses - that's all. But at that crucial moment, Aunt Harriet opened the stair door and stood aghast. I don't quite know how you stand aghast, but she was definitely doing it. *"Frank, Florence, what are you doing? I thought you were playing games!"*

"We are Aunt... I mean... we were."

"I think you'd better go home, Frank."

"Yes, Aunt."

Lower Hurdsfield - Fence Street from Dicken Street.

Lower Hurdsfield - Arbourhay Street

And without a backward glance I left her. I shall have to stop writing - I can't see for tears! They sent her packing the next day and got an older woman in..... and Grandpa died!

My word but that was a funeral. A horse-drawn hearse and coaches. To me it looked more like a carnival but that was because so many men formed the procession. No women attended the funeral at all.

After the service in the house, the coffin was carried out and followed by my father and his four brothers. They formed up in front of the hearse with father in front, then Fred and Jack paired and Harry and Arthur paired. I was bundled into the first coach first (protocol, of course; the eldest of the eldest), then young Fred (son of Fred) and Jack (son of Arthur).

There were two grandsons in the next coach who by seniority should have come before Arthur's Jack, but because of Salic Law, by being the sons of daughters, they were put after the sons of the youngest of Grandpa's children. Yes, it does sound complicated, put like that.

I remember looking through the window of the coach before we started and was amazed to see the length of the procession; it almost reached Buxton Road bridge. I said to Fred, the elder, *"Who are all these men?"* Being older than I was and more knowledgable, he replied (rather airily I thought) that Grandpa was such and such at the Chamber of Trade, and as a Town Councillor, etc. *"Didn't you know?"*

After that silence reigned in our coach and it seemed to take hours to get to the cemetery. The year was 1929 and I was 14.

One day Father said, *"We have arranged for you to start work."* This took me rather by surprise because I had forgotten I'd 'left' school during a period of sickness. *"Oh"*, I asked. *"Where?"*

"Well", Mother took up the tale, *"before I married your father I used to go out with a girl called Pattie Orme, and she married Edmund Lomas who owns a silk mill on Waters Green. We have talked it over with both of them and they think it would be a good idea if you started to work in the office there, and you would be learning the trade along with their son Geoffrey. What do you think?"*

After the initial shock I felt rather sad, because work had never entered my head until now. *"No"* I pronounced rather weightily, *"I don't want an office job"*. So the subject was never mentioned again.

Part 6: Hard Labour - and the Penalty

My decision not to accept employment at Edmond Lomas' mill was probably the silliest I ever made in my life, as future events showed; but I was determined to go it alone.

If I couldn't stick to music - I never asked if I could (the implication was I should find a job) - then there were to be no half measures. I went to see Mr George Rushton of Enoch Rushton and Sons, Engineers, Davenport Street, and got myself fixed up. When I told my parents they were not as pleased as I expected them to be.

"But that's a dirty job," said my mother. *"And you'll have to wear overalls,"* said my father.

The dream of their son entering management had gone now. *"Still, if that's what you want - and you were always good with your Meccano,"* said my father with a twinkle in his eye.

But the decision had its musical link, because Harold Galley, who sang the bass arias of my favourite Messiah and played the violin to my piano accompaniments, worked at Rushton's.

I shall never forget my first day at work. After a kindly talk with Mr Rushton Snr, I was shown the job I had to do. There was no messing about, like fetching and carrying for someone. I was thrown in the deep end and put to work on a lathe, drilling ³/₄" holes in castings for 'spinning frames'. It wasn't particularly the work that got me, but the standing in one position. Every now and then I felt faint and only the grip on the 'boring wheel' saved me from ending up on the floor. I just about lasted out until 6 o'clock that evening.

But as the days went on I got used to standing, until it didn't bother me at all. My wage for the first 12 months was to be six shillings a week. I was lucky to get anything at all, really, Mr Rushton explained to my father, as most apprentices paid their bosses for the knowledge of the trade!

Work went on and I learnt what I was supposed to learn. And other things as well.... It was an all-male establishment - not even a girl in the office - so I suppose it was natural that a lot of swearing went on among the men, and I picked it up, as I picked up smoking, and thought no more about it. This was a very strange fact because I had never heard a swear word at home and I was deeply involved in Church and Sunday School work, so how I caught the habit is a mystery. Lack of thought, I suppose. Until one day someone made me think. The man's name was Fred Wyatt and he was the side-drummer in the Bethel Band (Macclesfield's star silver band in those days).

To this man I have ever been grateful - just how much I suppose he never knew. One day he must have spoken to me about something and I must have come out with a swear word in reply because he got hold of me by the scruff of the shirt front and said very fiercely, *"If I ever hear you swear again I'll knock you into the middle of next week! What do you think your parents would say if they heard you?"*

From that day I've never uttered what is called a four-letter word and when I think back there is a great string of them - some quite common in both Chaucer and Shakespeare. So that was the answer to one bad habit of mine - shock treatment. There were two other men on the shop floor who didn't swear and they were the aforementioned Harold Galley, the singer and violinist, and Jack Mathers, who was a member of the Parish Church choir.

From Jack, who was always singing in a good bass voice, I learned to sing the very arias which I accompanied Harold in, and I always looked forward to working on the machine next to his, so the time I spent working at Rushton's wasn't entirely wasted as I at first thought.

One day they took me home and put me to bed, with what Dr Anderson at first thought was a dose of 'flu but which turned out to be a leaking heart valve. The year was 1930. The explanation seemed to be that I had put too much effort into 'striking' for the blacksmith at the forge (a part of every engineer's workshop). All apprentices had to get used to this job, which meant perhaps ten or a dozen strikes at a time with the sledgehammer raised above your head until the blacksmith turned the piece of metal over, and then you started all over again. And being out of breath was no excuse - come to think of it, it was like being on hard labour in prison! So ended my dream of being an engineer.

This illness took an important chunk out of my life, from the age of 15 to 19, with two years practically all the time in bed plus two years' convalescence. These were the years when a normal healthy lad learned a trade and knocked about with others of his own age. But here I was, paying for my folly. The doctors had warned years before - no games to be played - no bikes to be ridden - and when I left school, no heavy job. I was undone!

As I have said before, music had taken firm root in my soul long before this and it helped very much now. I had a gramophone and a wireless set in

Arbourhay Street from Blagg Street.

Hurdsfield - Gladstone Square.

Frank's father and mother.

my bedroom and when some work of interest was being broadcast I would switch on. The gramophone was more difficult as it had to be wound up, but my Aunt Harriet came in handy here because she enjoyed the task, especially if it involved her beloved Handel. And so the time passed.....

Doctors came regularly (before the days of National Insurance) and a heart specialist came from Manchester to shake his head. That must have cost 10 or 20 guineas! It wasn't livened up either by having three parsons visiting regularly. Mr Madgen came from my own Park Green Chapel, Mr Wintersgill from my father's family chapel in Sunderland Street (Wesley's Chapel) and as we were in the parish of St. Paul's - and I was a past pupil of that school, Mr Thetford, the vicar, was very attentive indeed.

As I got better I asked for a dummy keyboard to be made in wood, and this was produced, about two octaves in length, but being without sound it wasn't a great success. Attempts were made to gear it up to a table-size harp which someone produced, but again (hardly surprising) it didn't work very well, although I learned to strum on the harp itself.

Then, one day, John Fred Mellor, the auctioneer at Brocklehurst's salesrooms, turned up with his wife's mandolin. This was indeed a help, for as it was tuned like a violin and played with a plectrum, it cut out the awkward bowing.

I wrote much music; in some books it was the well-known melodies I wanted to play, and in others, various original themes which occurred to me. One particular hymn tune got its 'first performance' by the Park Green choir a few months after it was written. During this time Mr Madgen, our loveable seraphic-faced minister, left town with his family to take over another church, and in his place came the Rev. W. J. Teague. who hailed from Northampton way and Mrs Teague from Bude in Cornwall. Although Mr Teague hadn't the M.A. degree after his name like Mr Madgen, he was the more highbrow type, liking music and drama, and in the pulpit a real theologian. He was with us when the New Methodist Hymn Book was published in 1932, and when everyone had been supplied with one, he got the congregation (or most of them) to stay on after the evening service every Sunday for a 'Hymn Sing' to learn the new tunes.

Part 7: Back to Sunday School

With two years practically all the time in bed, plus two years' convalescence, I could at least claim that I had tried to prove them wrong in my attempt to be an engineer.

I won through in the end because when they diagnosed a leaking heart valve they said it was just a matter of time. It wouldn't heal (there were no plastic valves in those days). When I finally recovered, Mr Thetford, the vicar of St. Paul's, hailed me publicly as a living miracle. Shouted it out, he did, in Mill Street!

1 must say that their prayers probably did far more good than the doctor's medicine, because this only seemed to be the usual red tonic stuff. So prayer, coupled with the will to live - helped enormously by music - pulled me through this trying time.

And most of my thanks, of course, I owed to my mother who nursed me through what must have seemed an eternity to her, especially as she had a shop to run too. She saw to my every need, and her fervent prayers were added to the many others, for besides the bedside devotions, I understand that the three ministers asked for the grace of God to be given to me from their respective pulpits.

After my first two years I was allowed to potter about the bedroom and get dressed, so that I could now wind up my own gramophone and was able to do a bit of violin practice, although I found this very tiring at first.

It was on an evening in 1932 - I remember I'd got into bed early, feeling tired - that I heard my Grannie coming upstairs. She had just called to me as usual that she was coming up to bed when she suddenly collapsed halfway up. Mum went to get Dad from the other shop and Uncle Harry came along too and they got Grannie to bed while Mum ran round the corner to get Dr Cootes.

Mrs Cooper from next door came to stay with her while Mum was away and I went in to them. Mrs Cooper said simply, *"She's going"* and no sooner had she said it than Grannie had gone. It must have been a great shock for Mum when she rushed in with the doctor to find her mother dead.

I don't remember much more about the incident as I was bundled back to bed and I seemed to stay there until after Grannie's funeral; she was 73. But gradually things got back to normal - for me at any rate - but they could never be the same again for Mum as she had lost Grannie's help in the shop, and still had me to cope with, Dad being in his own shop till 8 and 9 o'clock every night.

My Grannie came from a long line of 'Bumblies', that is to say that the family were very respectable working class. My Great Grandfather Hulme (Grannie's maiden name) was a hand-loom weaver and carried on his trade in the garret of a house in Canal Street, off Green Street. They were 'respectable' because their lives were tied up with Park Green Methodist Sunday School and the Chapel, but they were 'Bumblies' because they never seemed to think for themselves. Whatever they heard or whatever you told them, they would believe. This I suppose, is the natural way of such a family. They never quarrelled or criticised anyone. They were nice people.

Grannie had a sister Alice whose married name was Barnes. She had five daughters and they lived in Lyon Street, off Bond Street. They all worked at Clapham's shirt mill, Athey Street, just round the corner. The eldest and youngest Lizzie and Emily, never married. Lily married when she was about 40, an Anglo-American named Jim Hurst. Emma married a Co-op tailor named Will Dean, of York Street off Buxton Road; they had two sons, George and Ernest. Pattie married an engineer from Chesterfield, named Arthur Williamson; they had two sons, Harold and Arthur.

Grannie's brother, John Hulme, had two sons and four daughters. Harold the eldest had a son, Harold and a daughter Dorothy. Ernest had no family and lived at Denton.

The eldest daughter (another Pattie) married Fred Bennett of Landsdowne Street. Next came Laura, who married Ellis Tebay, a stone mason; they had two daughters, Madge and Phyllis, and the two younger ones remained unmarried. When Pattie died, these last two - Edith and Lily - moved in with Fred, to house-keep for him.

As my health improved I could go down to the piano in Mrs Cooper's house next door. She was glad of my company. Whether she was glad of my everlasting piano playing I am not too sure. Harold Galley was still visiting the house and I looked forward to the evenings when he brought along his violin and his voice which had improved to a rich baritone. His repertoire was quite good also, from oratorio and opera to folk songs and the popular ballads. My own taste too was widening from Handel to Bach, from Haydn to Mozart, from Schubert to Beethoven, etc. Brahms came much later - Wagner not at all.

I took up playing the piano at Park Green Sunday School again and became a regular attender at both morning and evening services, enjoying the duties of being door steward again.

The social side of church life had been sobered down quite a lot since the amalgamation of the United Methodists with the Wesleyans. Gone now were the days of the Social, Dance and Whist Drive. It was even a sin now to hold a raffle, whereas before I was ill everybody had been raffling everything! The Sunday School was 'graded' into departments, secretaries, treasurers, and all the paraphernalia of beaurocracy installed. A Miss Hart from Sutton Coldfield was engaged to put everyone through their paces and to establish a weekly study group for teachers. A Wesley Guild was started up, with its attendant secretaries, and for a time I did the Devotional one.

The only people who stuck out firmly against all this change and absolutely refused to be 'graded' or to take any part in the rest of the Sunday School activities was the Young Men's Class, ably led by Fred Bennett, who must then have been approaching retirement age.

It remained under his stern guidance an entirely separate entity and we were referred to as *"Them down there"* and they were *"Us up here"* up being an odd room upstairs somewhere.

We had, by way of diversions, recitals, all very uplifting for the few, but for the many not very exciting. Freda Johnson, who had studied with Louis

Kentner, would play a piano solo, then Willie Mottershead a violin solo or Alex Young a cello solo, then one of the Ashton brothers, or both of them, would sing; Doris Wellings would recite. Essie Wellings had a nice voice, and Doreen (Willie's sister) would sometimes play the final piano solo.

Freda also held her pupils' concerts in the school, and they were always enjoyable. The annual Sale of Work was retained by special dispensation of the Wesleyans, but it wasn't the same *"without them there raffles."*

Mr Hayes the organist retired and his place was taken by young Ken Thomson, a brilliant young player, and then he moved on and John Barnes took the job. His inexperience showed up rather after Ken's playing, but he put in plenty of practice and duly became competent; so much so as to become, in later years, deputy to Dr Thalben-Ball at Methodist Central Hall, Westminster (Dr Lloyd Webber became choir master in John's time and when the latter left London to return to Macclesfield as Managing Director of Hovis, another local boy took over the organ; Leonard Lee of Rowan Way).

Part 8: A shop - and a car - of my own

When I was 19 my father had a brilliant idea. He bought me a shop to run. *"It's in the music line, so it should suit you,"* he said. This was the premises at 44 Sunderland Street previously owned by Albert Breese Snr and run by Albert Breese Jnr. They were jewellers and owned another shop in Sunderland Street, and had decided to put young Albert in charge of that business. So I took over a shop that wasn't in a strict sense 'musical' except that we sold radio sets and gramophone records, but the bread and butter was the sale of batteries, both wet (accumulators) and dry, Exide types, for the running of the radio sets. We also stocked new bicycles, which was quite a good summer trade; in fact, we once sold a tandem.

Father wasn't interested in the project after he bought it because I never remember him coming into the shop at all. The staff consisted of Marjorie Morlidge behind the counter and Joe Goodwin, a radio service mechanic (Mrs Cooper's son-in-law who gave up his shop in Lowe Street to join us).

I was also set up with an old Morris 12 car but the petrol consumption was so bad that I only kept it about six weeks. Norman Allen, Cookson's salesman, took me out for driving lessons but on Wednesday half-day closing day father paid a transport driver - Tommy - to come out with us on runs to Wales and the Lakes, so that after the six weeks I was ready for a test.

Now, the driving test had just been introduced and my appointment coincided with the change of car. We had a Morris 8 in place of the old Morris 12. In those days,you had to travel to Levenshulme where the examiner met you outside the Library, and the test began there. Then you proceeded through Ardwick to Piccadilly, turned right up Oldham Street into Oldham Road, then left onto the Bury Road; left again into Deansgate and left into St. Peter's Square and along Moseley Street back into Piccadilly - no one-way in those days.

There you parked and the examiner asked some questions (Norman Allen was still with us in the back of the car, listening intently no doubt). Then we drove back through Longsight and left for Belle Vue. On a quiet stretch of the Hyde Road we did the reversing procedures and the 'three point landings', then drove back to Levenshulme and the test was over. After one or two more questions came the eagerly-awaited pronouncement: *"Well lad, you've passed, but just watch those hand signals a bit more. Good day!"*

About this time, our collie sheepdog, Jack, went blind and we had to have him put down. We also had a younger Old English sheepdog called Bill who was run over by a lorry outside the shop and had his leg in plaster for a fair while. Both dogs were never allowed by my father to put a paw inside the house - they were working dogs, not pets, so they had a kennel each outside and in the colder weather they bedded down in the stable.

Bill got over his broken leg nicely but my father had to go into hospital for a stomach operation. He must have been in for four or five weeks and all the time we noticed that Bill had gone off his food. He got thinner and thinner until he was too weak to move and finally died the day before father came home.

While my father was in hospital I talked Mother round into helping me buy a bigger car. The Morris 8 was all right, of course, but lacking in comfort, and more important, lacking in speed. In fact it was flat out at 55 mph. We traded it in at Gleaves for a Triumph 'Gloria' which was a year old. My, what a car! A very low, sleek, semi-sports job, with inflatable cushions - and speed. Why, given a good road (few and far between in those days), you could get 85 mph!

Father wasn't very pleased when he found out that Mother and I had 'connived', as he put it, to change cars; the other would have been far more economical to run, he said. However, when he was well enough to have a run out, he was very pleased. Mum, Dad and I went out somewhere almost every Wednesday afternoon after we'd closed our respective shops. Considering

Above: A 1935 photo of Frank's radio and bicycle shop in Sunderland Street on the corner of Pickford Street. Frank's Triumph 'Gloria' is parked to the side. The shop became Blackshaw Bros (Merchants)

Frank aged 19 years, just recovered from his long period of sickness and reunited with his beloved violin. 1934.

Frank's Triumph

that it must have been 2pm by the time we started off, we covered some ground, particularly in the summer. A favourite run was through Llangollen and the Nant Ffrangon Pass to Caernarfon, and then back by the coast road, Llandudno, Colwyn, Rhyl, Chester, and back home by about 10 pm. Another run we especially enjoyed was up to the Lakes as far as Keswick and Derwentwater and back around Coniston. Mother always packed the picnic basket and the accessories to go with it.

I think perhaps this cramming of enjoyment was the reaction to those four anxious years of my being cooped up with illness. I felt free at last.

I'd been going round with a lad called Reg McKinnell who lived round the corner from us. I've no idea how the association started because he was a Catholic, so school was ruled out. He may have run errands for Mother. This was most likely because she had everyone at it, including Stan Turner, Wilf Dean and Harry Cooper. Anyway, we used to go to the pictures as lads did, and then one Sunday I asked him to come to Park Street Chapel to listen to Handel's Messiah, for me an occasion not to be missed. He flatly refused, and then he said, *"You see, if I come with you there, I should have to confess to our Priest."* *"Why?"* I asked. *"Because we are not allowed, as Catholics, to enter a Protestant building."* *"But this isn't a religious service,"* I protested, *"it's just an Oratorio."* *"Sorry,"* he replied. *"It would be a sin."*

My next pal was Ted Hulse, who had just started to teach in the Sunday School, so we had quite a bit in common as he attended the weekly study group. He enjoyed and shared my flair for speed in the car although he continually joked that I'd be "done" for it one day.

As it happened, that day came when he wasn't with me, but my parents were. I fancy we were on our way to the Lakes again. It was a well-known stretch of road to me, this side of Wigan. Some fool had put 30 mph limit signs up since last time and I hadn't noticed them. A police car was in wait, gave chase and flagged me down. I dropped my window and innocently asked what was the matter.

"Speeding" came the reply.

"But there's no limit on the road," I countered.

"Oh yes there is. See your driving licence, sir?"

"But it isn't a built-up area." said Father. *"This is open country.'*

"On that far side, yes." said the officer, *"but then there's homes on this side. Insurance?"* He walked leisurely round the car and took the number. *"I*

shall have to summons you, sir, for doing 42 miles an hour in a built-up area."

"But," said Mother, "it was my fault, you see, Constable, I asked him to pass the lorry in front of us."

"No use, madam: 42 miles an hour." He gave me a slip of paper.

"You'll be hearing from the court when you have to appear."

"At Wigan?" I asked. "That's right, sir, good day."

"Well, I ask you. 42 mph. I wouldn't have minded if I had been speeding!" Ted laughed loudly when I told him. "It's all right for you," I told him, "you don't have to appear." At that he just rolled about. After he'd subsided a little, he said: "Neither do you - get the RAC to send a solicitor." Ted wasn't in a solicitor's office for nothing. Yes, of course, that's what I paid a membership fee for, wasn't it? So I wrote to the RAC and they dealt with it, but I had to pay a £2 fine. I was found guilty, of course!

THE END

Postscript by Geoffrey

Despite Frank's sickness throughout his childhood and teenage years, he was passed A1 for the Army at the commencement of hostilities in 1939 and remained in apparent good health during his war service. On leave from the Royal Army Service Corps in 1941 he married his sweetheart, Margaret Kellett. He served with the 8th Army in North Africa, Sicily, the Italian mainland and on to Austria where he saw service with the Royal Air Supply Corps. On leave in 1945 he saw his daughter, Jean, aged two and a half, for the first time and was demobbed the next year. In the following years he and Margaret were blessed with two further daughters, Paula and Gillian. He was employed mainly by Brocklehurst Whiston and towards the end of his working life by Cheshire Tobacco, Jordangate.

Devoted to his family, the church and to music, this gentle and unassuming man was a prolific writer of hymns and music and for many years reported authoritatively and sensitively on local musical events for the Macclesfield press; he also wrote a novel and several plays.

Following his war service his life was again blighted by ill-health, a legacy of his boyhood rheumatic fever.

He died 30th December 1996, aged 81.

SOME LOCAL BOOKS FROM CHURNET VALLEY

DOWN THE COBBLED STONES   John Lea £ 7.95

EARTH MYSTERIES OF THE THREE SHIRES   Doug Pickford £ 7.95

ANSON COAL & GAS MUSEUM Compiled by Ray Maddocks £ 4.95

BATHS AT BUXTON SPA Mike Langham and Colin Wells £ 9.95

BIDDULPH PLAYERS 1950-2000 Margaret Fernihough £ 9.95

BOOTHS OF DUNHAM MASSEY David Eastwood £ 9.95

DEVONSHIRE ROYAL HOSPITAL Mike Langham & Colin Wells £ 9.95

CELTIC WARRINGTON & OTHER MYSTERIES SERIES Mark Olly £12.95

COUNTRYWISE SERIES Raymond Rush £6.95

DRIVEN BY THE DANE   Tony Bonson £20.00

FOOTLOOSE IN THE PEAK Peter Clowes £ 7.95

MEMORIES OF GLOSSOPDALE Mollie Carney £ 9.95

LAND OF THE ETHEROW Neville T. Sharpe £ 9.95

HISTORY OF MACCLESFIELD 1817   John Corry   £16.95

MACCLESFIELD AT WAR Philip McGuinness £ 9.95

MACCLESFIELD DEMOLISHED - WELL REMEMBERED Raymond Maddock £ 8.95

MACCLESFIELD MAN: Memoirs of a pig-headed Maxonian Raymond Maddock £7.95

TROUBLED TIMES: Macclesfield 1790-1870 Keith Austin £ 9.95

MACCLESFIELD:FOR KING'S & COUNTRY - WWI DEATHS David Hill   £15.95

MANCHESTER CHILDRENS' HOSPITAL Pamela Barnes £ 9.95

NANCY, HURDSFIELD GIRL Memories of Macclesfield £ 6.95

HISTORY OF PARKSIDE HOSPITAL David Broadhurst £ 9.95

PEAK DISTRICT YEAR: What's on, Who's Who & Why on Earth   Paul Sullivan £ 8.95

PEAKLAND PICKINGS Neville T. Sharpe £ 7.95

THE PEOVER EYE John Lea Limited edition hardback £14.95

TIME FOR CHANGE John Lea £ 7.95

TIMPERLEY BOY Peter Scott £ 8.95